Hulings

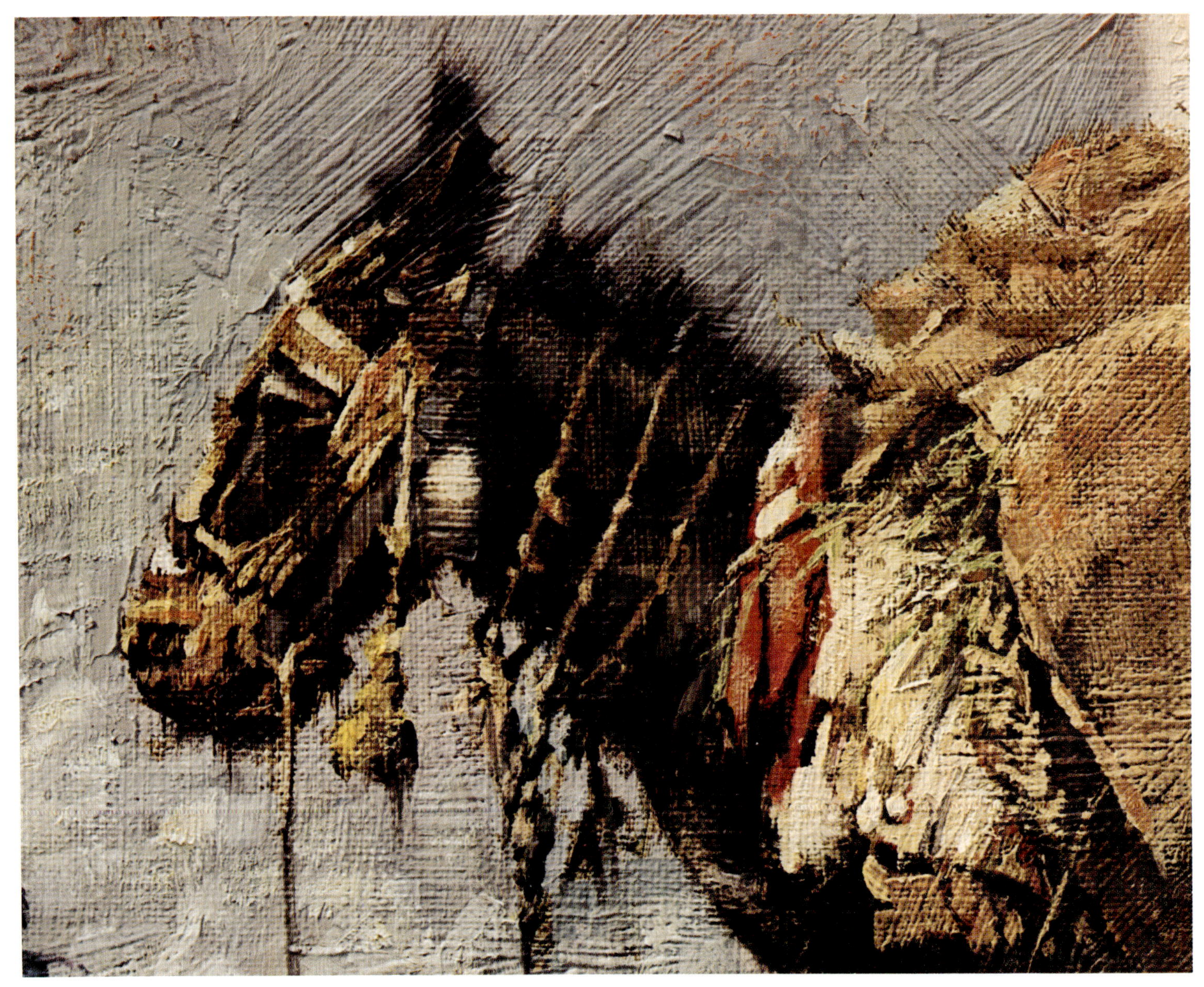

Detail from Plate Eight

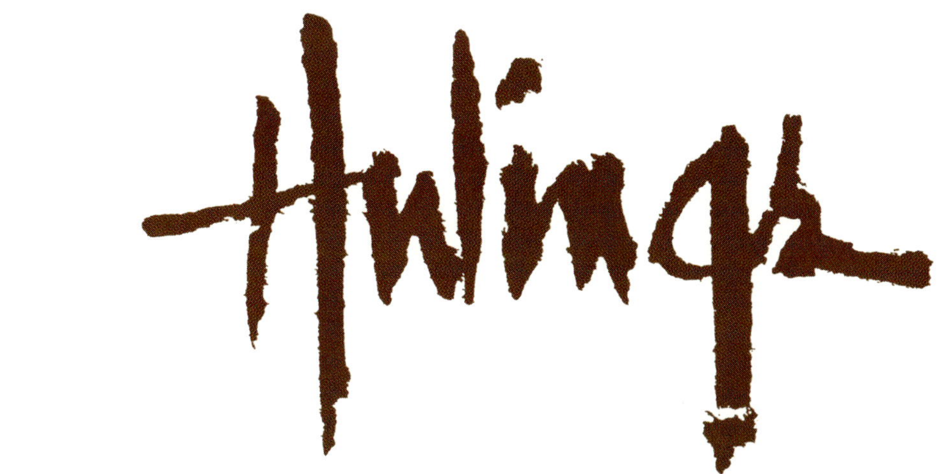

A Collection of Oil Paintings by Clark Hulings

The Lowell Press / Kansas City

FIRST EDITION

L.C. 76-21158 ISBN 0-913504-37-8

Printed in the United States of America

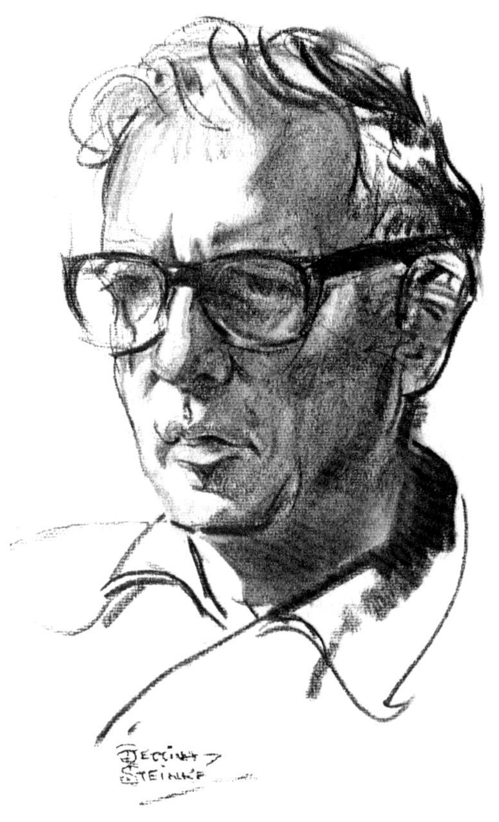

FOREWORD

In this collection, Clark Hulings broadens his scope as a Western painter in two basic ways. The more obvious one is that he has sought and found many of his pictures in the ancestral origins of "the West," namely in Mexico and especially Spain. As we know from the very language—rodeo, lariat, ranch and so on—this is where the American West came from. Hulings reports on its present status; if those old men with burros or those farmers threshing wheat in a manner unchanged over centuries don't look much like Tom Mix or Hoot Gibson (they may look a little more like Warren Oates) they are nevertheless cousins of everyone in the cowboy culture, descended directly from the same system of working the land with the help of animals that, mixed with the American character, the coming of the railroads and the consequent making of a market for beef, produced our West. As a Western painter, Hulings in these pictures is going home; the admirer of Western art will be happy to go along with him.

But Hulings is broadening his base in quite another way as well. A Paris flower market or pastry shop, after all, have nothing whatever to do with the West. And a pitcher full of roses might be taken, by some, as the very opposite of what Western painting is all about.

If those roses were so taken, that would be wrong. What Hulings is doing in this collection, essentially, is transferring the Western eye—an eye common to painter, collector, museum worker and simply resident in that part of the country—from its normal preoccupation with its familiar furnishings, vistas and people, to many other people and places. That there is such a thing as a Western eye is to me self-evident. It is formed, or trained, by the changing lights of the Western sky, by the vastness of the landscape, and also by the often crucial importance to the Westerner of being able to sense what the weather is going to do in the next half hour or half day. It is no accident that the overwhelming majority of these paintings are of outdoor scenes, that the principal interior, the "Blacksmith Shop," is of its nature a kind of adjunct to life outdoors and is lighted with great delicacy and modulation by the sun, rather than the industrial fire in the forge, which is just beyond the edge of the painting.

The Western eye of Clark Hulings developed in an unusual way. Two years of childhood in Spain put him in visual touch with the country of origin, as noted above, of much of the Western American culture. Then, after graduating from college as a physicist, he moved to Santa Fe to recover from illness. It was in Santa Fe, where he now lives, that Hulings began painting as a professional, supporting himself doing pastel portraits of children. His professional education continued in Denver, Louisiana and back in New York where his adolescence had been illuminated by visits to the Metropolitan Museum of Art. After some years of painting and wandering abroad, he settled again in Santa Fe, no longer as a newcomer but as a native returned. His Western eye is authentic and is enriched by his travels and sojourns in other countries and other regions of his own country.

Two superb examples of the Western eye of Clark Hulings at its most Western are "Tesuque Cottonwood" and "Taos Trees," both painted in northern New Mexico where Hulings makes his home. There is a European and Eastern American tradition of "the view," whether romantic, dramatic, sublime, whatever. Whole books have been written on "the picturesque," by which is meant scenery suitable to be painted in pictures. The notion is absolutely foreign to the Western artist, despite the presence in the West of some of the most extravagantly picturesque scenery anywhere in the world. Thus, there is nothing in the least picturesque about the trees in these two pictures. They are simply part of the on-going, overall Western land in which they grow. Hulings has found drama in the cottonwood by framing it and its golden bank of sunlight with the deep shadow of a bridge in the foreground, the ominous darkening of clouds and cloud shadow in the background.

It will be noted that you can count the pebbles in the foreground of that cottonwood; in contrast, the Taos trees are almost slap-dash sketchy in the paint application—except for the fact that the presence of the trees and their placement in space come through so forcefully: you could estimate the distance to those adobe dwellings on the right. That's one of the charms of Hulings' work: the style is not imposed willy-nilly upon all subjects that come his way; it is largely dictated by the subject—the light, the mood, the feeling of the artist about what he's looking at.

Try another pair of contrasts: those roses, observantly titled "Red and White Velvet," and the street flower market of "Paris in the Spring." The roses, seen in close-up, are loosely painted, yet painted with great feeling for the texture of the title; their background is so loosely painted as not to be there at all. Take away the roses and you'd have an abstraction and a quite presentable one; yet you have no difficulty knowing that the abstraction the pitcher rests on is horizontal, the abstraction behind it vertical. How different the flower market: the whole range of gladiolas, tulips and the rest is painted with meticulous attention to detail. It's not botanical painting—a special, too little appreciated branch of the art—but it's as close to that specialty as ordinary painting can get. Just as art dealers used to saw up Renaissance religious paintings into as many as a dozen saintly portraits per painting, so here you could saw up the flower stall into perhaps a dozen and a half—by my count—still lifes, each beautifully painted. Yet all of these flowers are composed into a single unity themselves. Also, they are part of a total composition or a pattern Hulings has found in completely different subjects. There is a slightly serpentine passage of the wet pavement between the flower stall and the tree on the rounded curb, a passage which takes in the distant buildings and ends in the moist sky faithfully reflected in the foreground puddle with which that passage begins. Hulings has painted this same passage in the canyons of his West and in the narrow Spanish streets in this collection. Incidentally, you have no trouble seeing that those roses were painted in New Mexico, the flower market in Paris: the light in the two pictures is intensely local.

But the eye is the same in both and that's the point. It is a Western eye, looking openly and inquiringly upon whatever comes to its attention, not seeking some "artistic" quality in the nature of the subject, but imbuing the subject with artistic value in part through the artist's mastery of his art, but in greater part through the sympathetic perception of his Western eye, which he can now turn anywhere to the pleasure and profit of all who see his work.

—Frank Getlein

Alexandria, Virginia

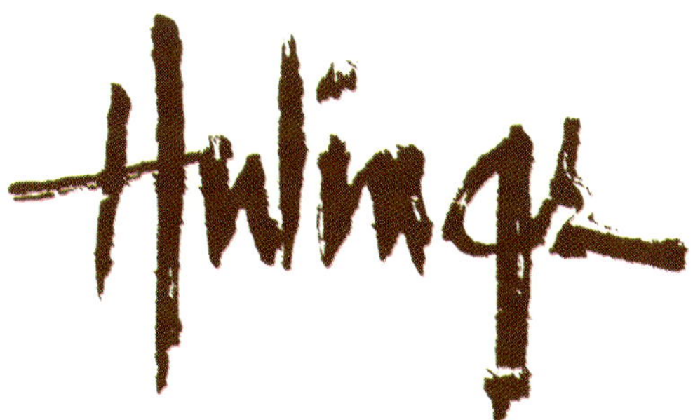

This collection is dedicated to my wife Mary and our little girl Elizabeth.

RED AND WHITE VELVET

"If you can paint a rose so that you feel it will tremble in a breeze, you need never be daunted by the texture of human skin." These words were spoken to me by my first teacher, Sigismund Ivanowski. That he said them during the Great Depression perhaps to justify our having roses to paint week after week, instead of human models who must be paid, in no way denies their validity. I regard roses as the most lovely and most difficult subjects and I will strive to meet Ivanowski's impossible challenge as long as I paint. Roses have both a firm structure that requires careful drawing and a delicate character that calls for loose, almost casual painting. And they wilt so fast!

Plate One 12x16 in.

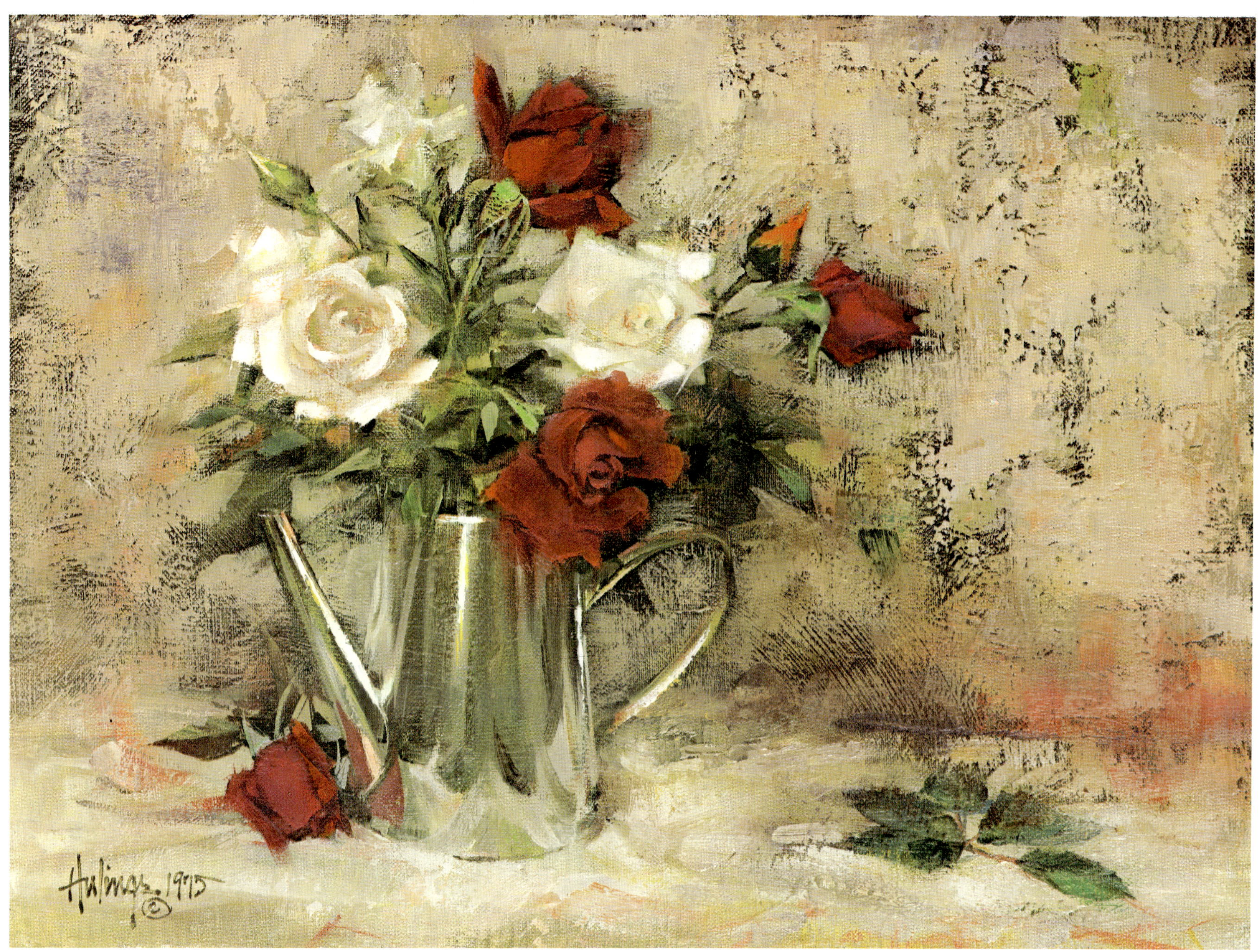

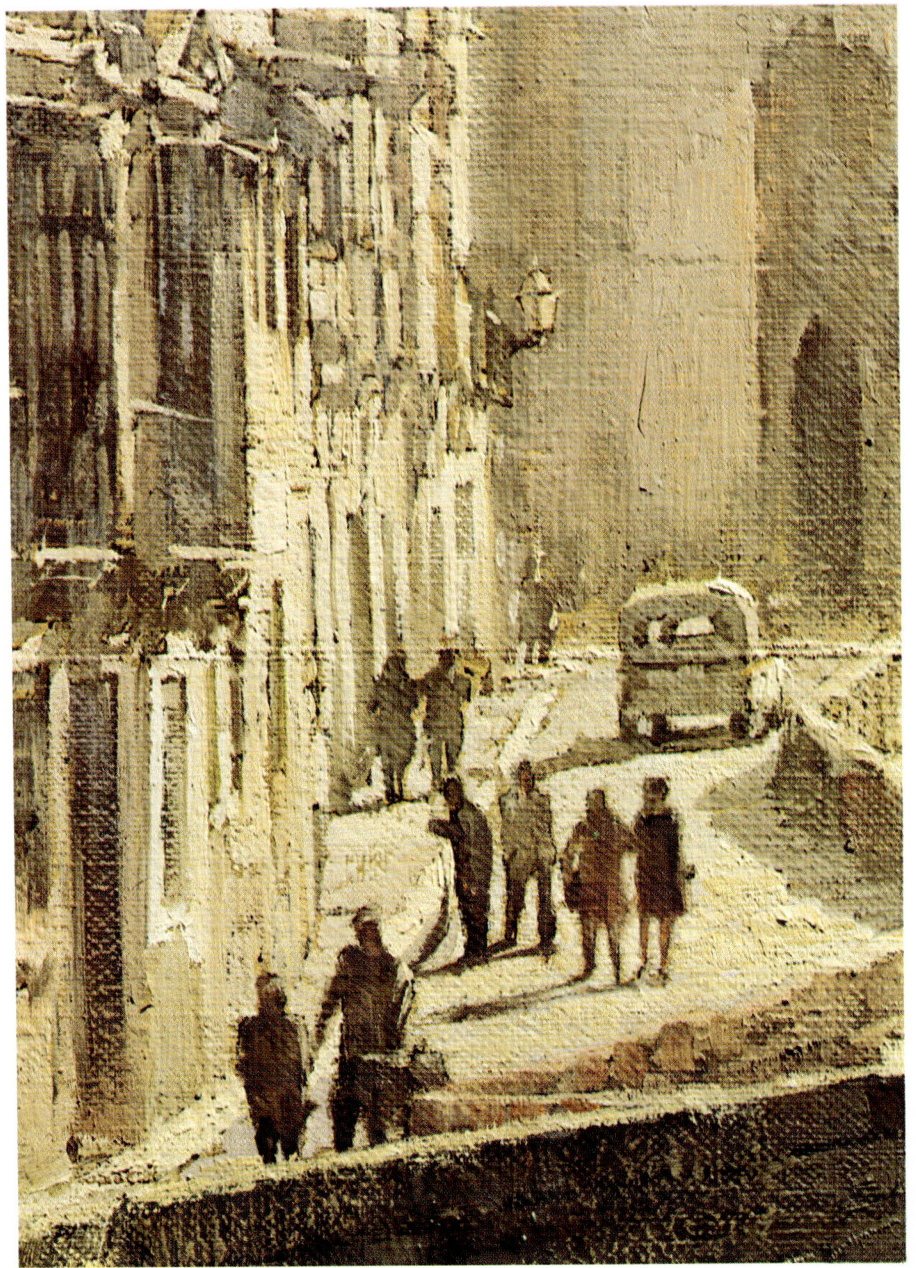

Detail from Plate Two

EARLY MORNING LIGHT, GRANADA

This ravine runs along the edge of the city of Granada, Spain. On the right, high above and out of sight, is the Moorish palace, The Alhambra. Directly ahead in the distance is the famous gypsy quarter. I have a special fondness for early morning light. Generally, there is water vapor in the air not yet burned off, and the sun is still low enough to produce long, interesting shadows. A facade of buildings at a glancing angle to the sun presents a staccato effect of shapes and accents. I like to play with a picture like this, putting everything in its place to achieve an atmospheric perspective bathed in cool, early morning sunlight.

Plate Two 32x48 in.

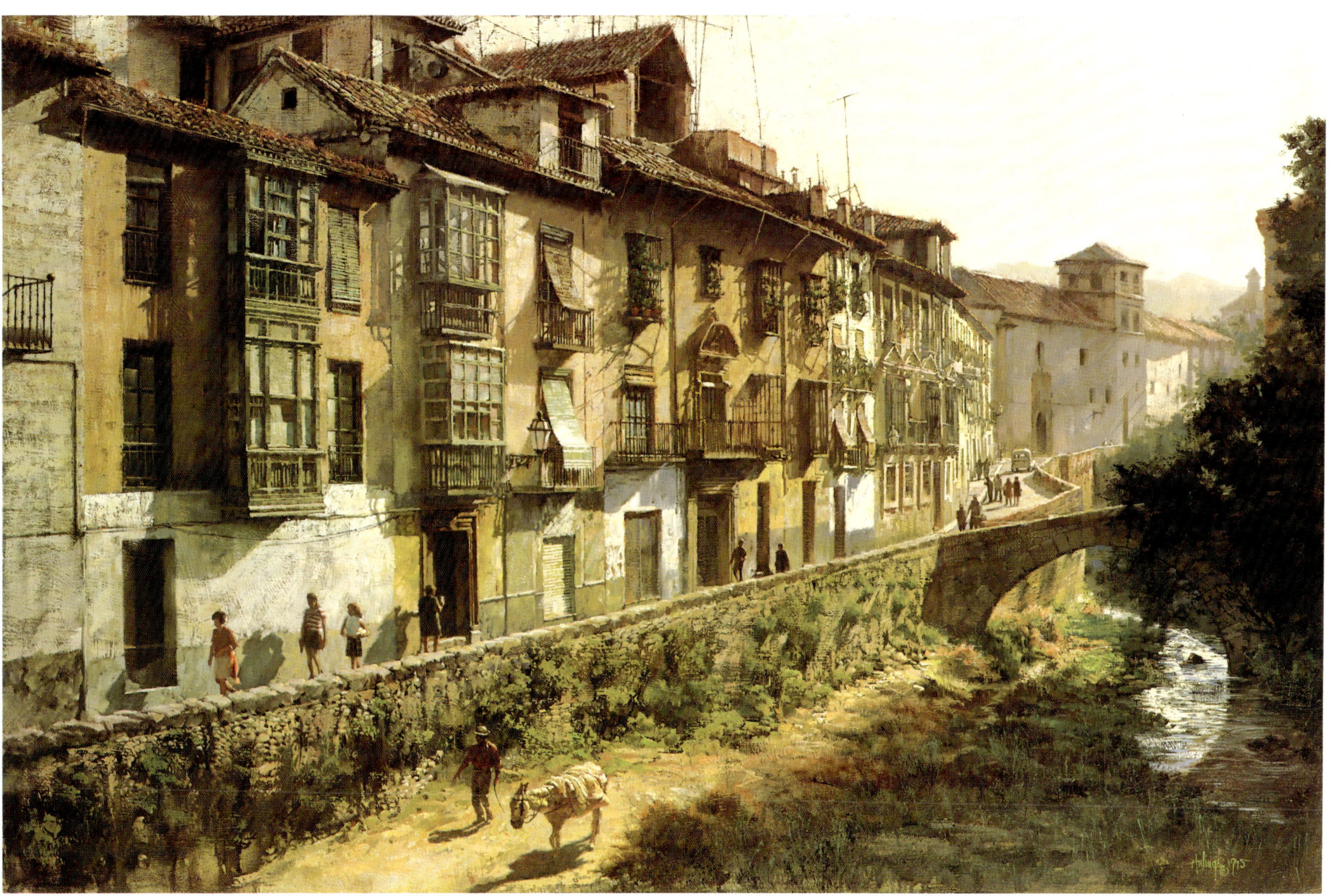

EL PALMAR, SPAIN—VIEW FROM THE BRIDGE

El Palmar is on a strip of land just south of Valencia amidst salt marshes and rice paddies. The sky is overcast. Good! Bright sun would destroy the softness of this pale olive light—and the fish wouldn't bite.

Plate Three 16x24 in.

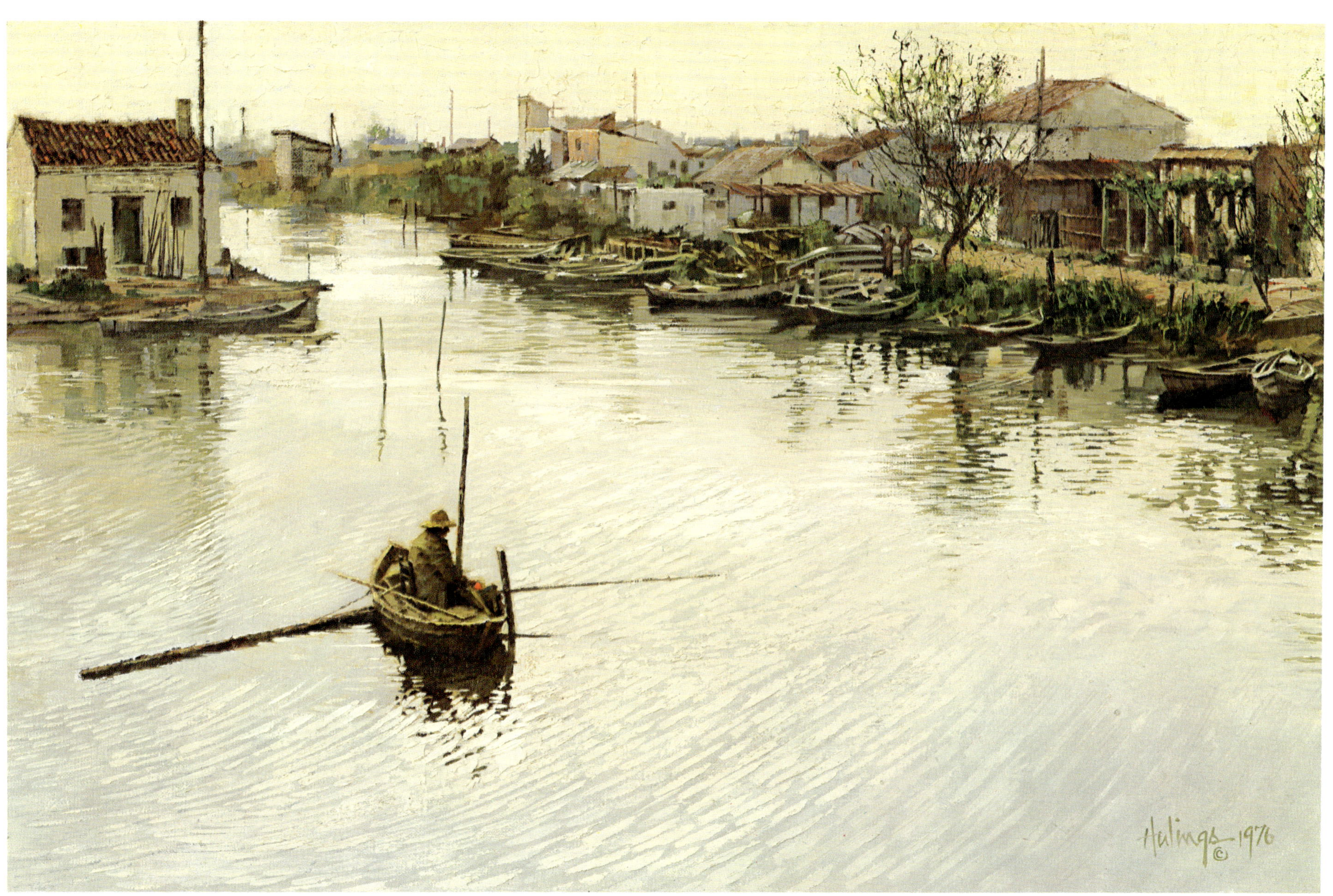
Hulings 1976
©

TESUQUE COTTONWOOD

Because of its high altitude, northern New Mexico enjoys a clear atmosphere. Sometimes when there is a background of dark, threatening rain clouds and a foreground bathed in bright sunlight, the effect is theatrical—arc-light theatrical. Here the effect is exaggerated because the scene is seen from beneath a bridge where it is dark—as in a theatre. It is good to paint from under a bridge because there is protection from the sun as well as cover from those dark rain clouds should they move into the foreground and carry out their threat.

Plate Four 24x36 in.

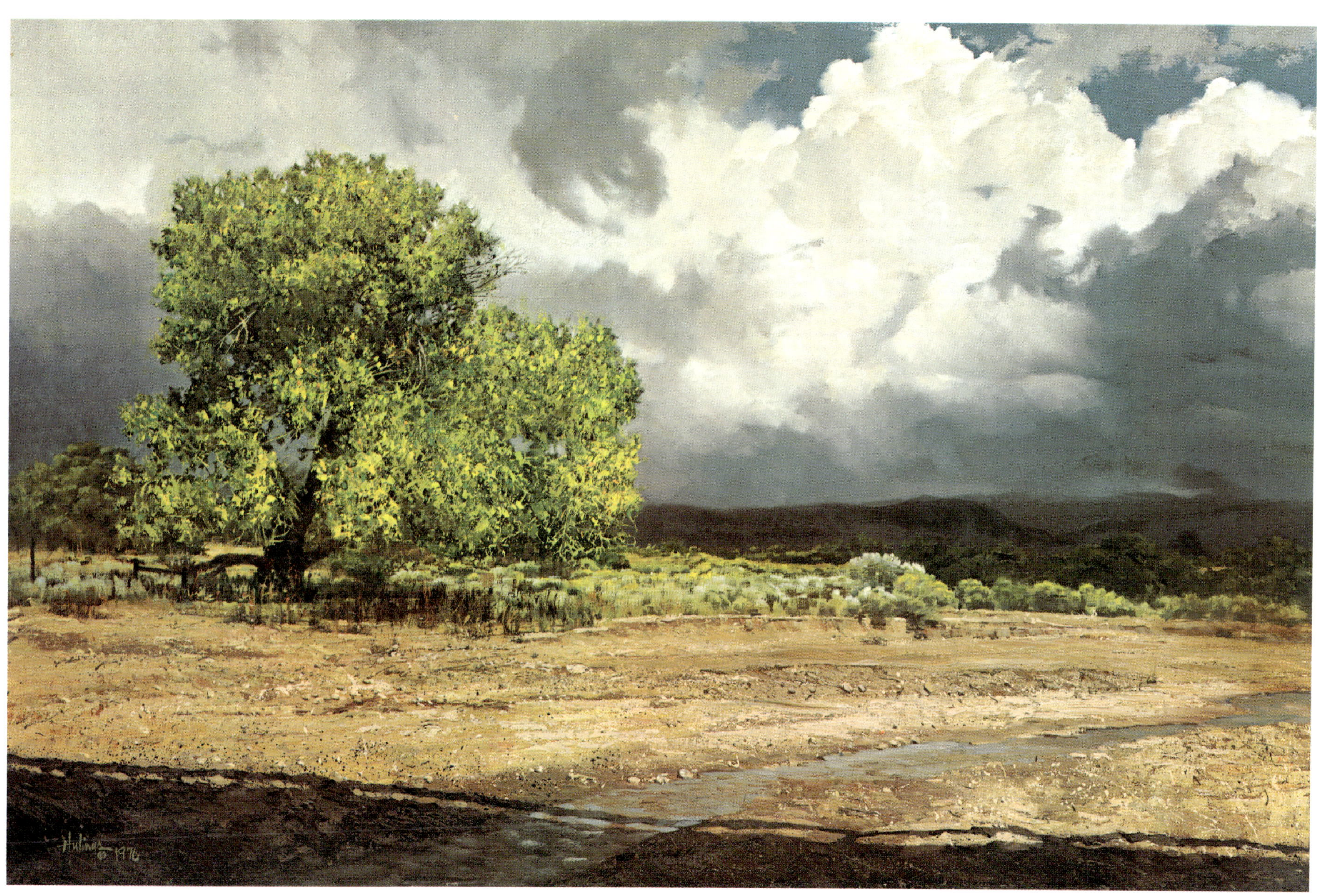

RANCHITO

Chapala, Mexico, is a fine place to sketch. The combination of simple white houses, lush tropical plants and intense blue sky is hard to beat. And there is the laundry on every line. At home in Santa Fe, electric dryers have denuded the landscape. My wife does not share my distress.

Plate Five 8x10 in.

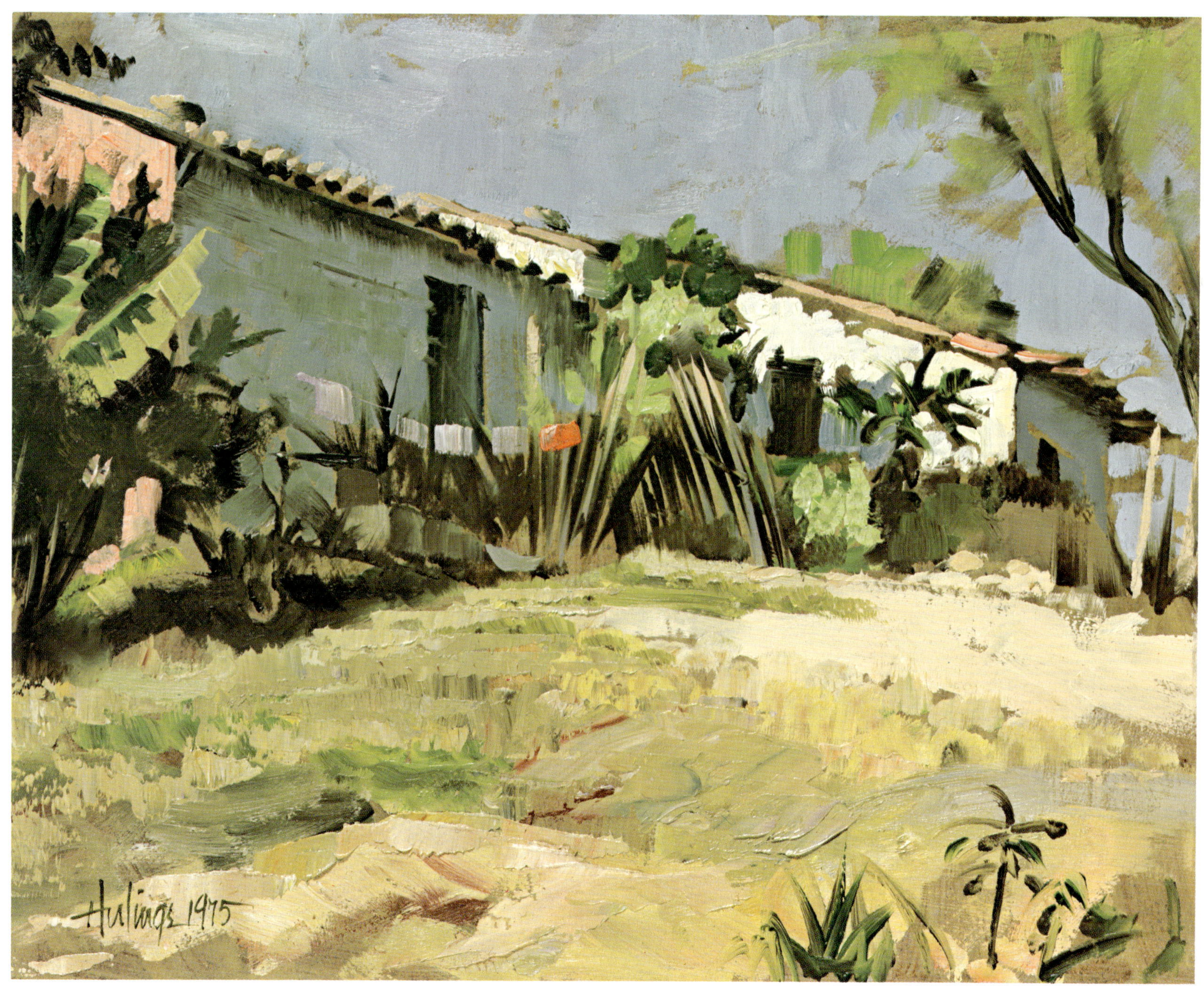
Hulings 1975

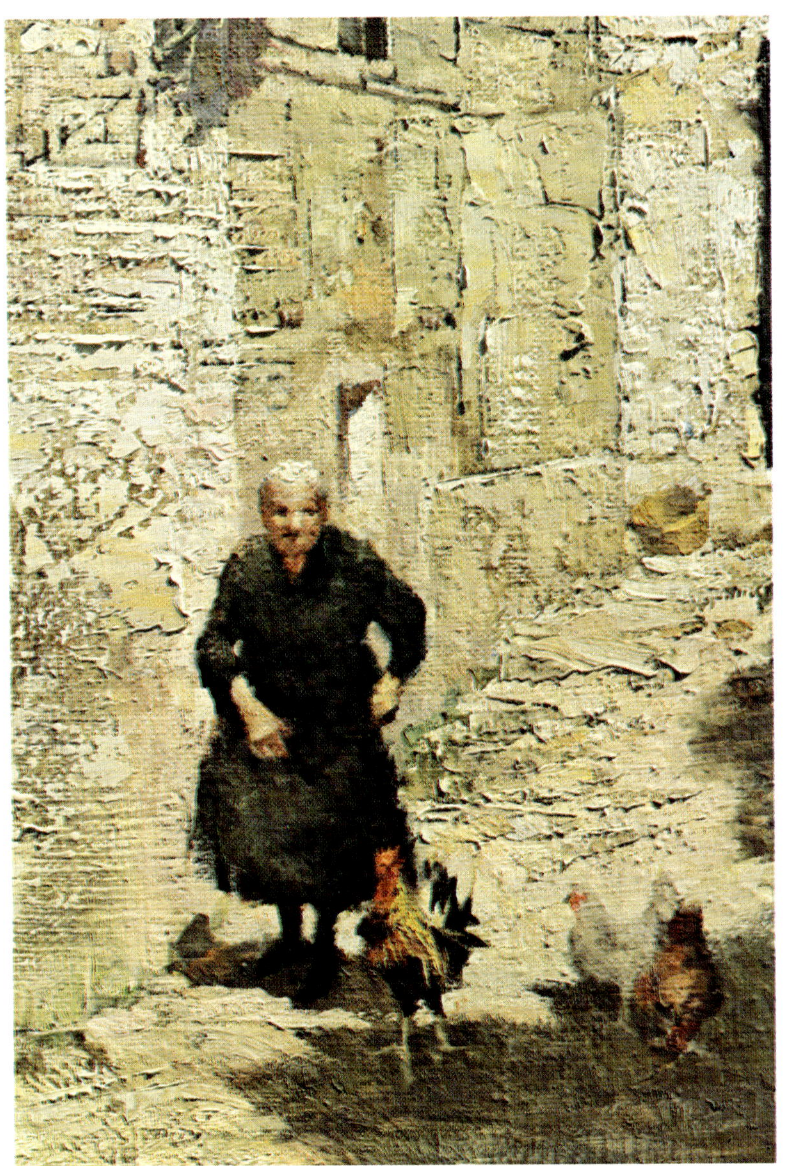

Detail from Plate Six

OLD WOMAN WITH CHICKENS

Those chickens wouldn't be allowed loose in the streets of today's Spain. But I must be indulged a nostalgic memory of my childhood when a drive through a string of villages was interrupted by at least one stop to pay for a run-over chicken. Old ladies in black still abound, but most of the younger ones have abandoned the tradition.

In civilizations older than our own a man protected his family and property with high stout walls. The streets were built as mere avenues of traffic. This severity is relieved by plants and vines sitting on upper story balconies and spilling over the walls from lovely gardens which we can only smell and imagine. But artists can be thankful for narrow passages that provide us with an occasional vertical composition.

Plate Six 27x18 in.

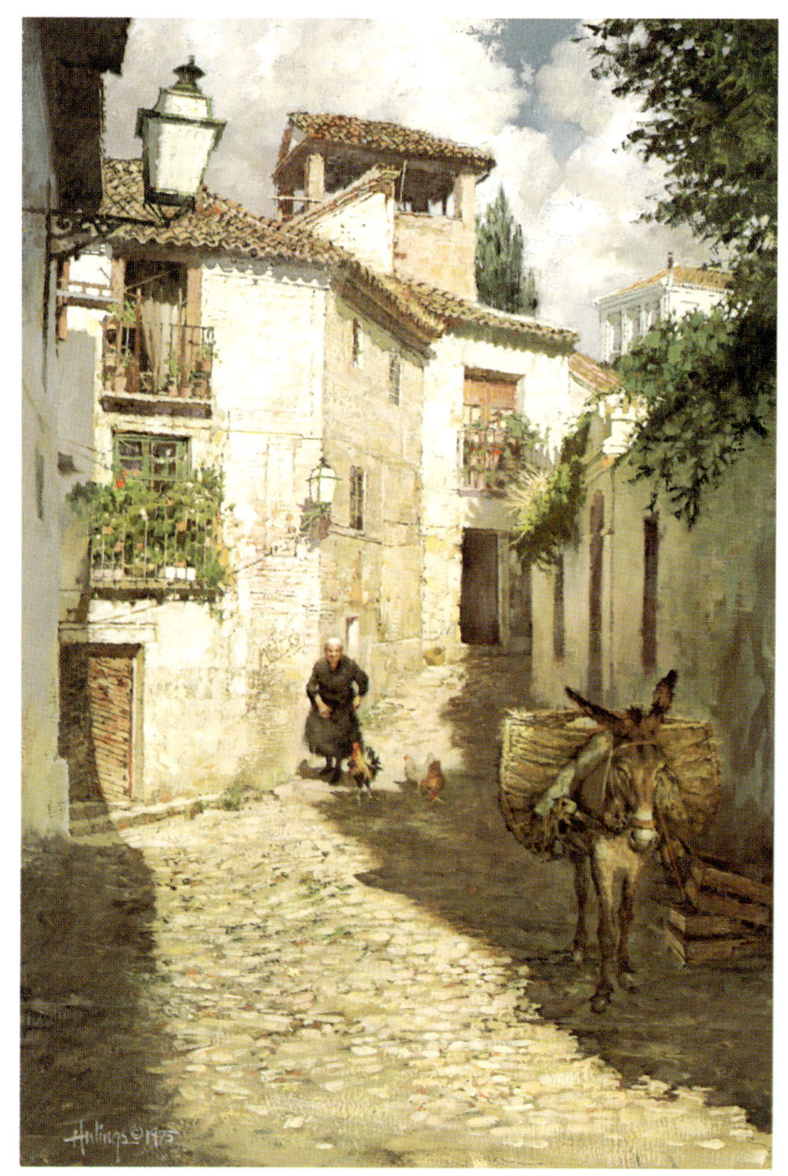

BLACKSMITH SHOP

This scene was interesting to me because of the flow of light from three sources—one emanating from the doorway in the picture, another from behind the viewer and yet another from the viewer's right. The challenge was to paint the figures and the still life objects so that they retained their identities while staying in place within the whole atmosphere.

This is not a "living room" picture. If you're painting something to be a sure seller, you don't choose the rear ends of an ox and some donkeys. It is the kind of painting that an artist paints just because he feels like it.

Plate Seven   21x34 in.

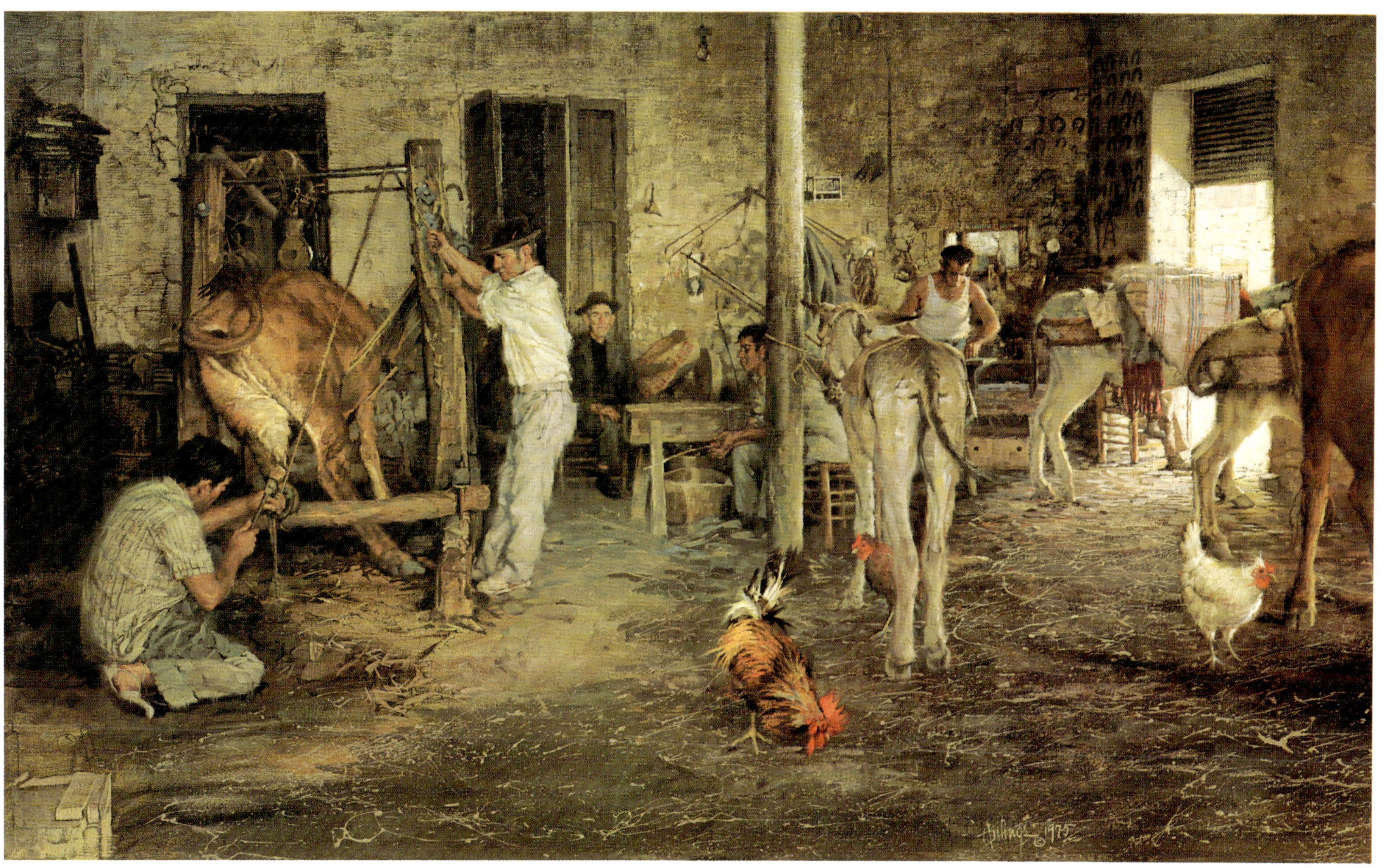

WATER TROUGH

When I was a very small boy we lived in a village in northernmost New York State. One of my earliest memories is watching people water their horses and mules at the trough near our house. The trough is still there fifty years later, but the animals are long gone. Too bad! For an artist, a pickup truck at a modern gas pump can't compare.

When I am in a country where animal power is still used, I like to plant myself near a water trough and let my subject matter come to me.

Plate Eight 12x18 in.

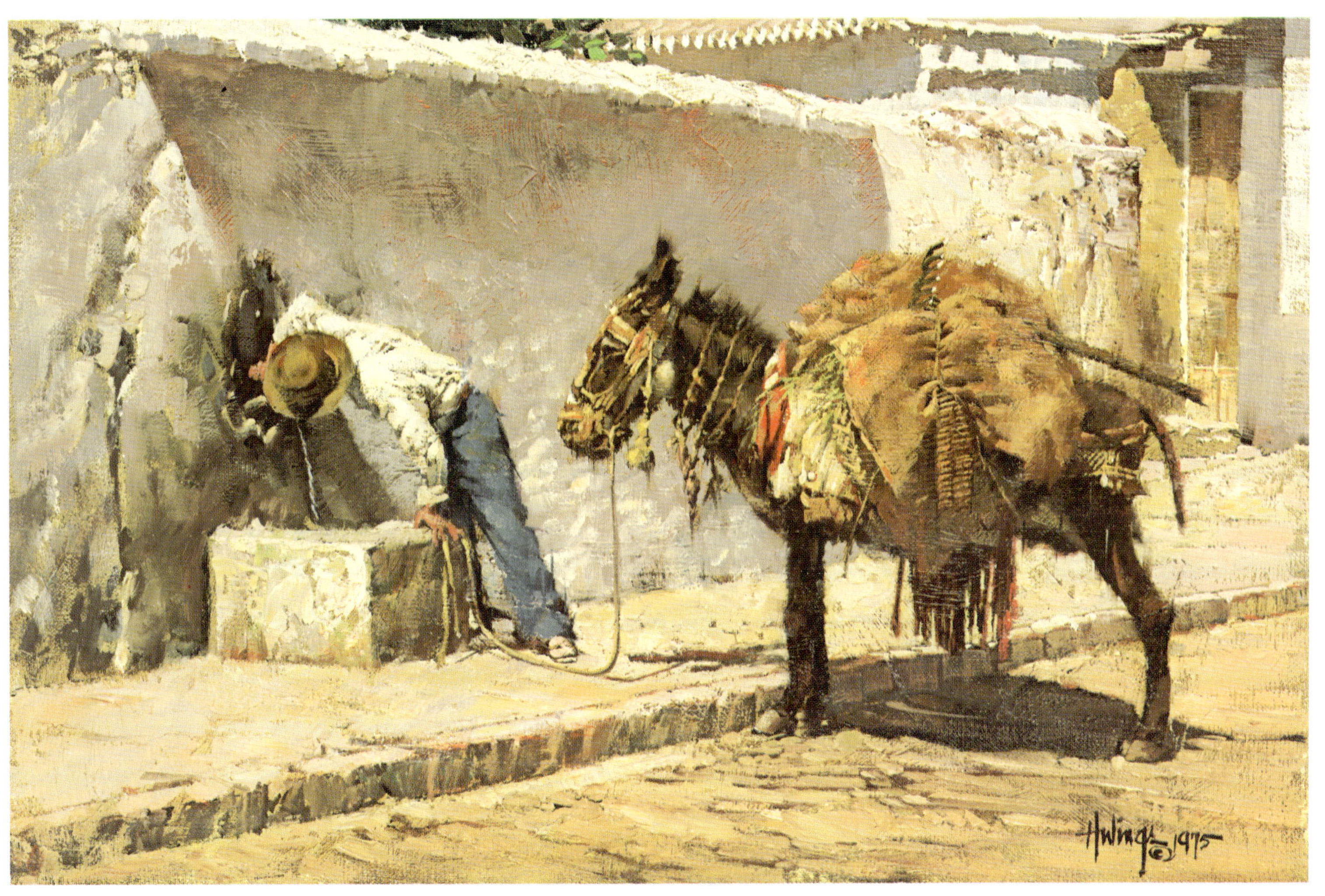

INDIAN STILL LIFE

I usually spend more time planning a still life than painting it. I begin with three times the number of objects that I will use. I like to have some kind of theme—or at least use items that are somehow related to each other. This painting contains things that were made or used by Indians. The figure is a Hopi social dancer doll, similar to a Kachina doll and made in about 1870. It's a very rare artifact made of cottonwood root. The blanket is Navajo and the bowl is a pre-Colombian relic from northeastern Mexico. To me, the fun of still life painting is in trying to capture the texture and personality of an onion, a tomato, corn, wool, etc., while creating a pleasing, harmonious picture.

Plate Nine 18x24 in.

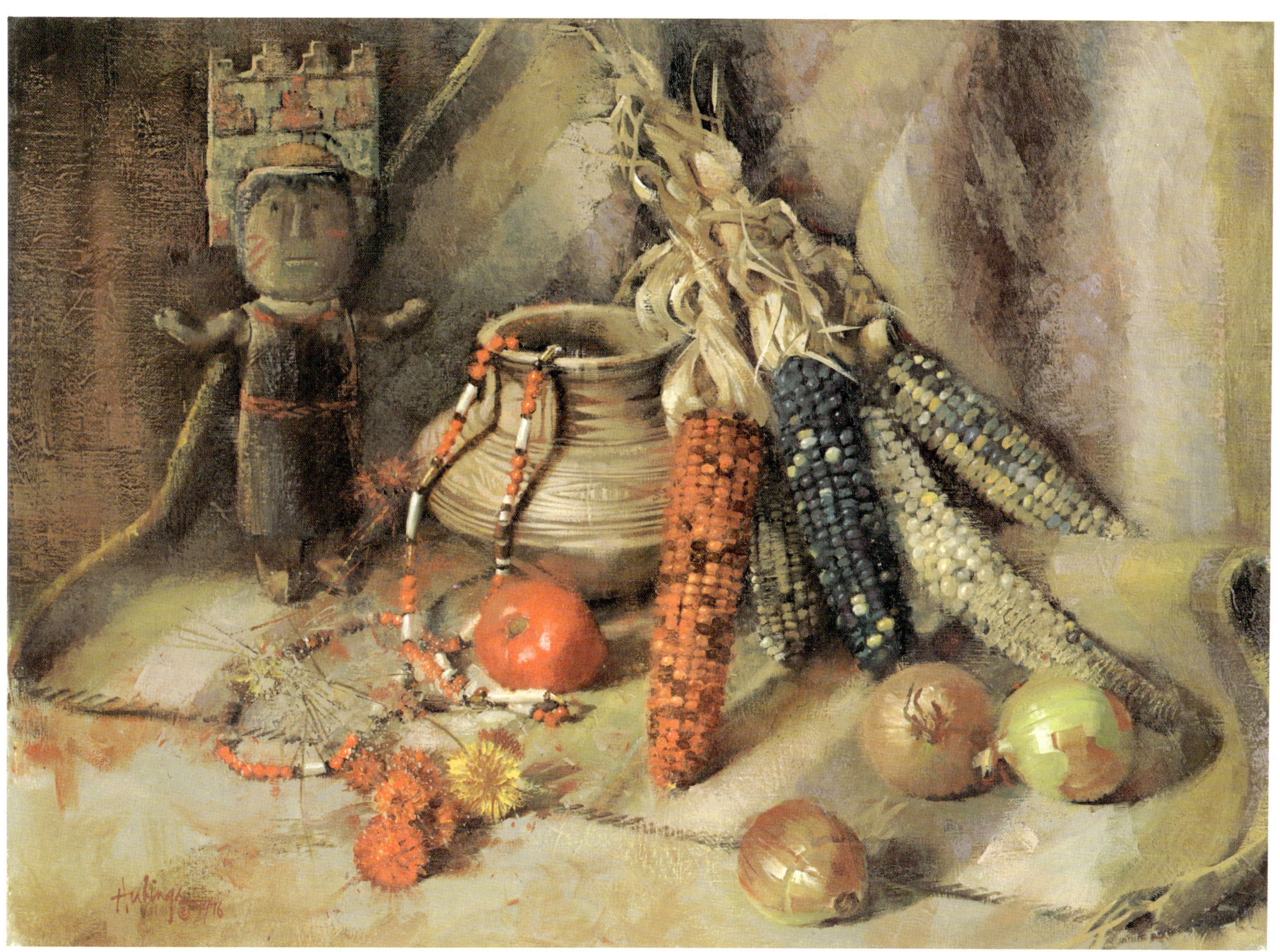

FRENCH RAGPICKER

The section of Paris where this boulangerie, or pastry shop, is located is possibly the most painted subject in the whole body of art. It is the Montmartre district where many celebrated artists have lived and painted.

The little tramp with his umbrella and satchel and long, ill-fitting coat is a poignant figure. The mood is reinforced by the sad gray Parisian light.

Plate Ten 16x24 in.

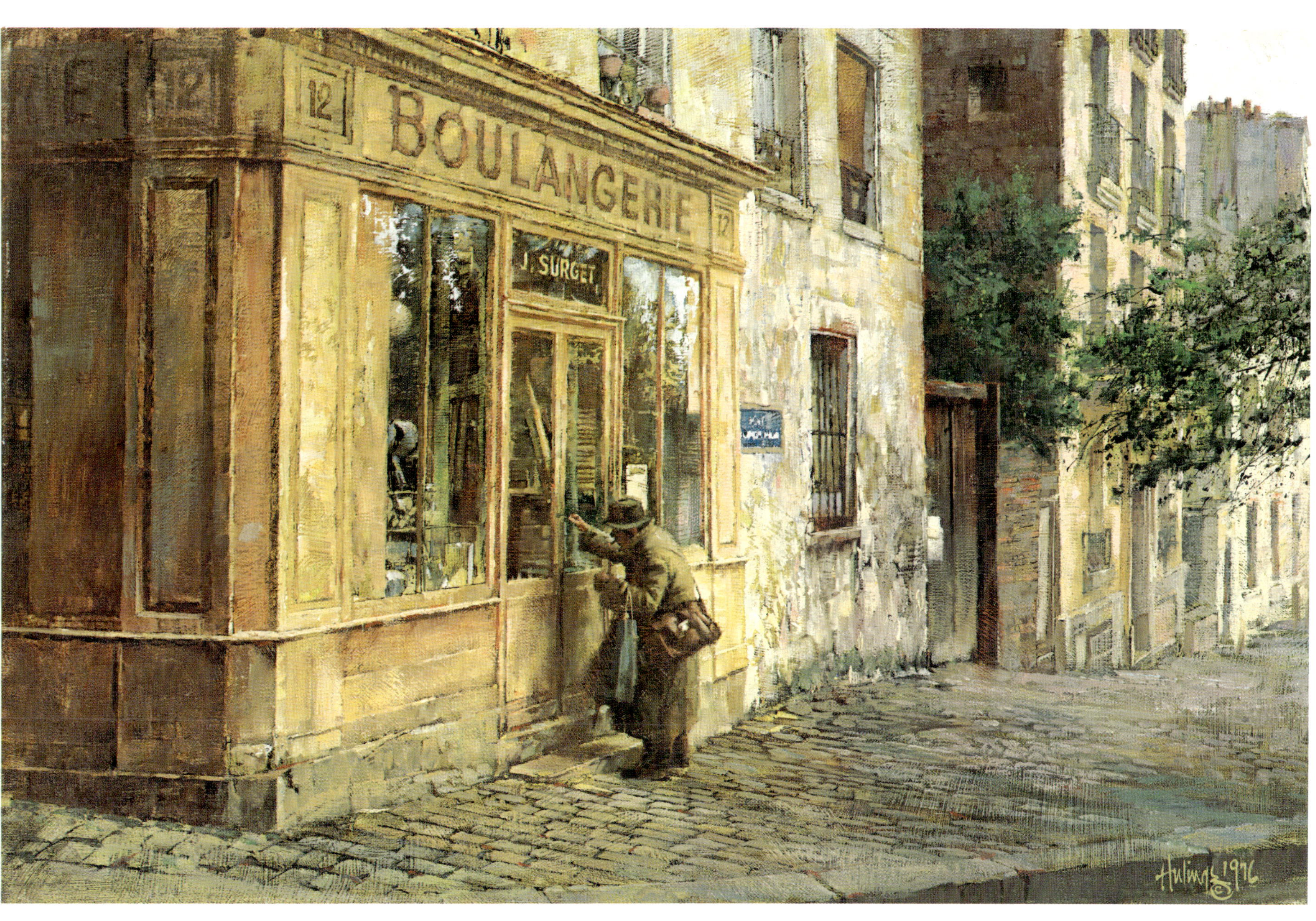
12
12
BOULANGERIE
12
J. SURGET
Hulings 1976

THRESHING WHEAT

Who knows how many centuries they've been threshing wheat in this manner in Spain? However long, there has always been the sunny warmth of the back lighting, the pattern of the white village on the hill and the texture of the straw.

A surgeon friend of mine with a great interest in painting visited my studio while this painting was on the easel. He wanted to know how the straw was painted. I said, "I splatter," and proceeded under his questioning to describe how I load a brush with paint of given consistency and hit it against a palette knife to produce the random texture of straw. When I had finished, I jibed him by saying, "In return for revealing this precious secret I expect no less than a ringside seat at one of your operations." He replied, "You will be most welcome—you know, we splatter too."

Plate Eleven 24x36 in.

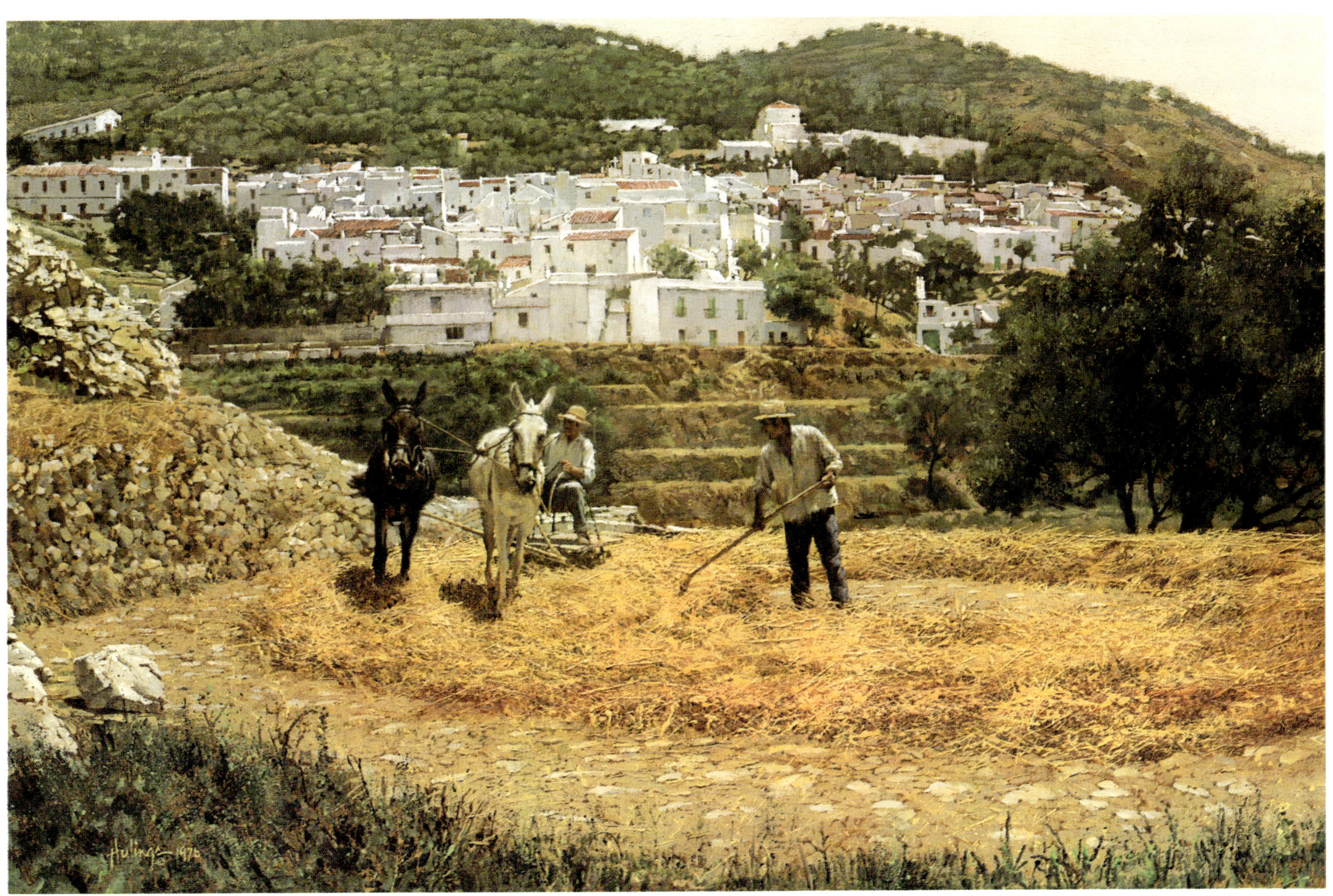
Hulings

WOMEN WASHING

In places where money is scarce and clothes are worn out before they are discarded, last year's party dress is this year's housedress. The lady on her knees at the scrubboard has tied an apron around her thighs to keep the fancy flounces out of the water.

Plate Twelve 16x24 in.

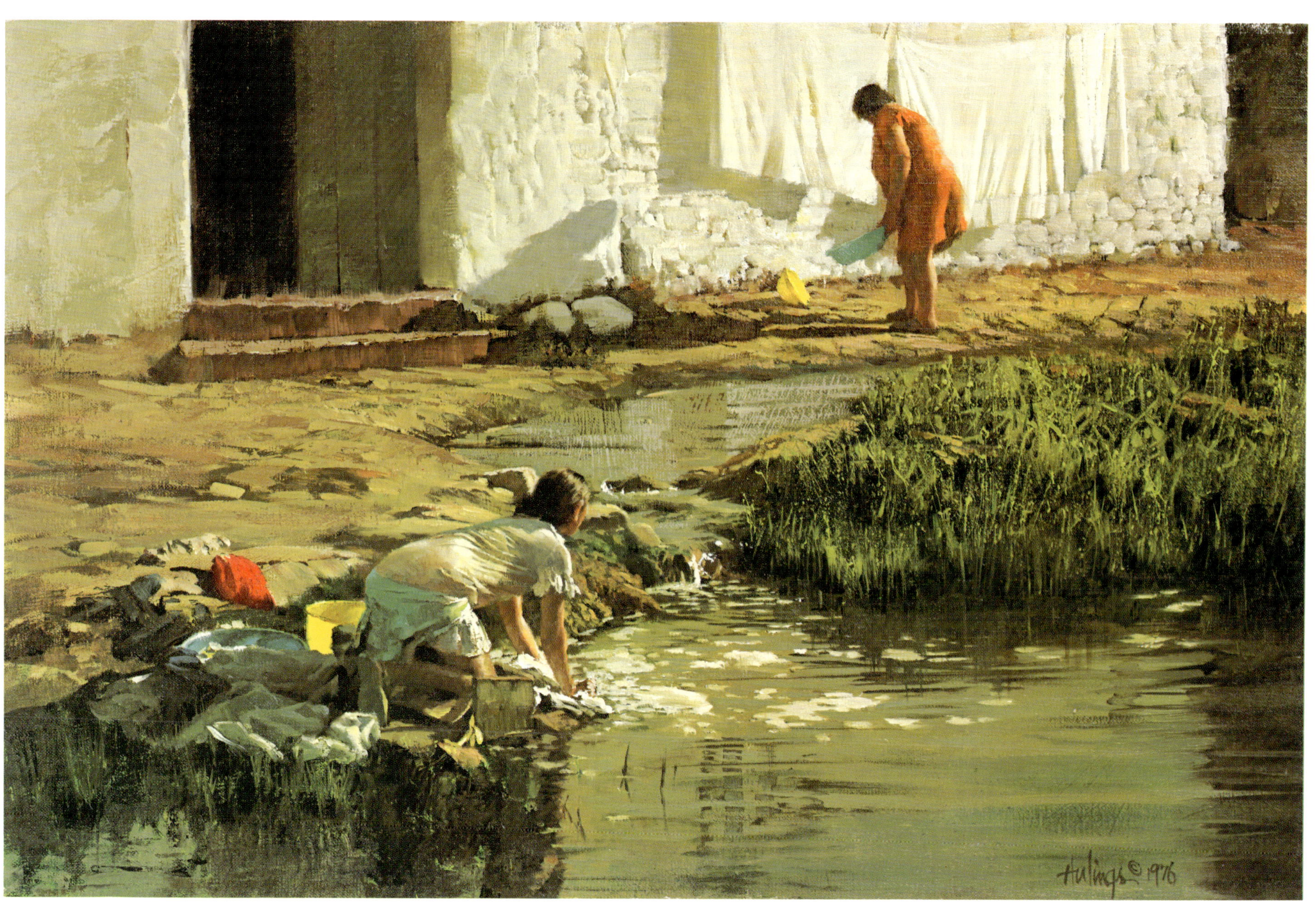
Hulings © 1976

BURRO WITH RED TASSEL

Some people have a need to beautify their surroundings, however humdrum or functional those surroundings may be. I see this in the intricate and esthetic designs of corn baskets and pottery made for everyday use by New Mexican Indians. I see it in brickwork patterns of a colonial New England kitchen fireplace. And I see it in the decorative trappings on this little burro. The red tassel on his brow is not always a tassel. Sometimes it is a carnation.

Plate Thirteen 16x20 in.

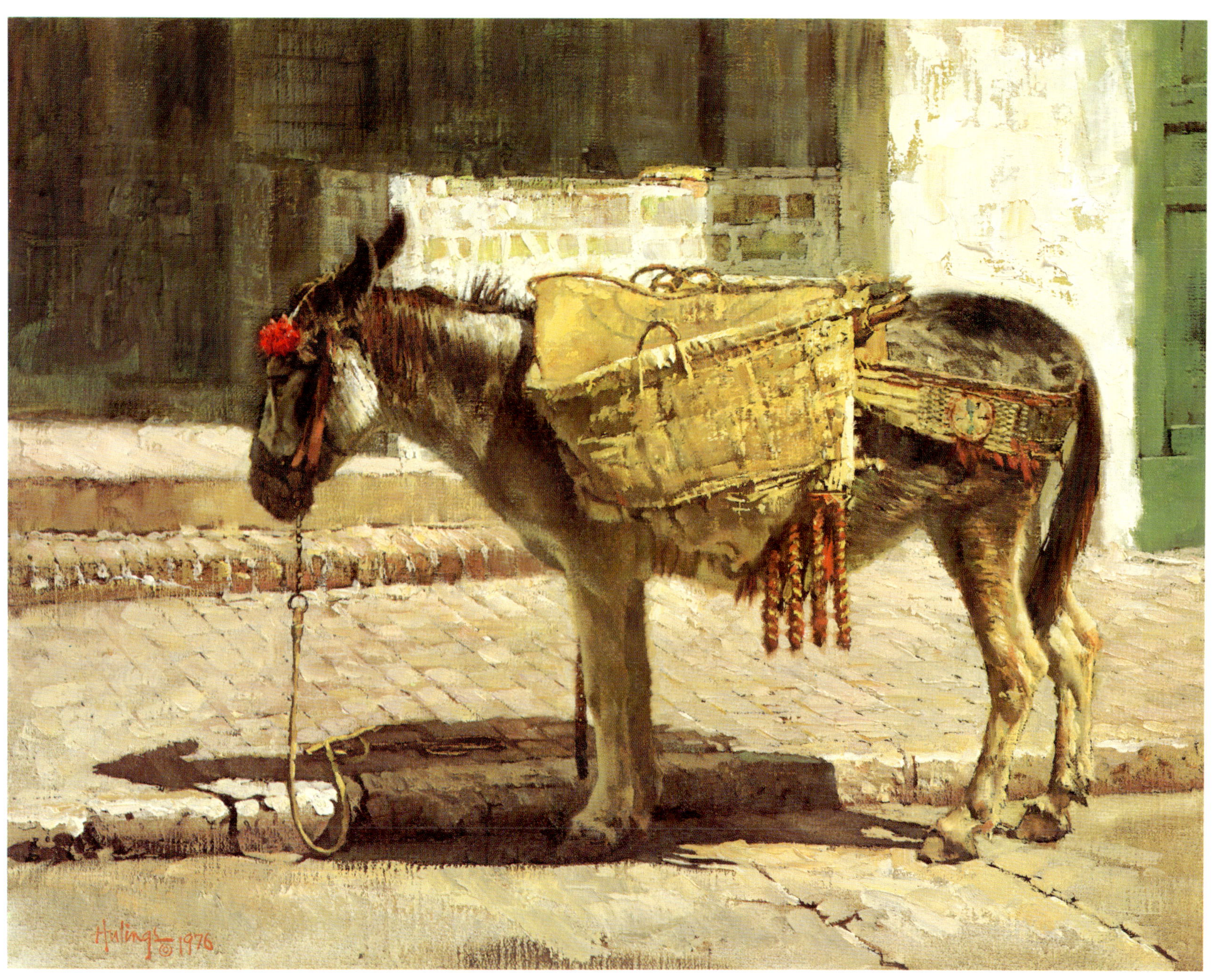
Hulings ©1976

JOE

I used to visit a plantation home in Louisiana where this man worked. He had always lived there, as had his slave ancestors before him. I was a young portrait painter and had been commissioned to paint the lady of the house. This required many trips and each time I arrived, the gate was opened for me by Joe. For some reason I kept calling him Jim and one day he decided it was time to correct me. With exquisite tact that some people are born with, he said: "I'se Joe—Jim ain't here."

The expression of sadness and dignity in his eyes made me wish I could paint him instead of the lady. I asked if I could take his picture and now, thirty years later, here is his portrait.

Plate Fourteen 20x16 in.

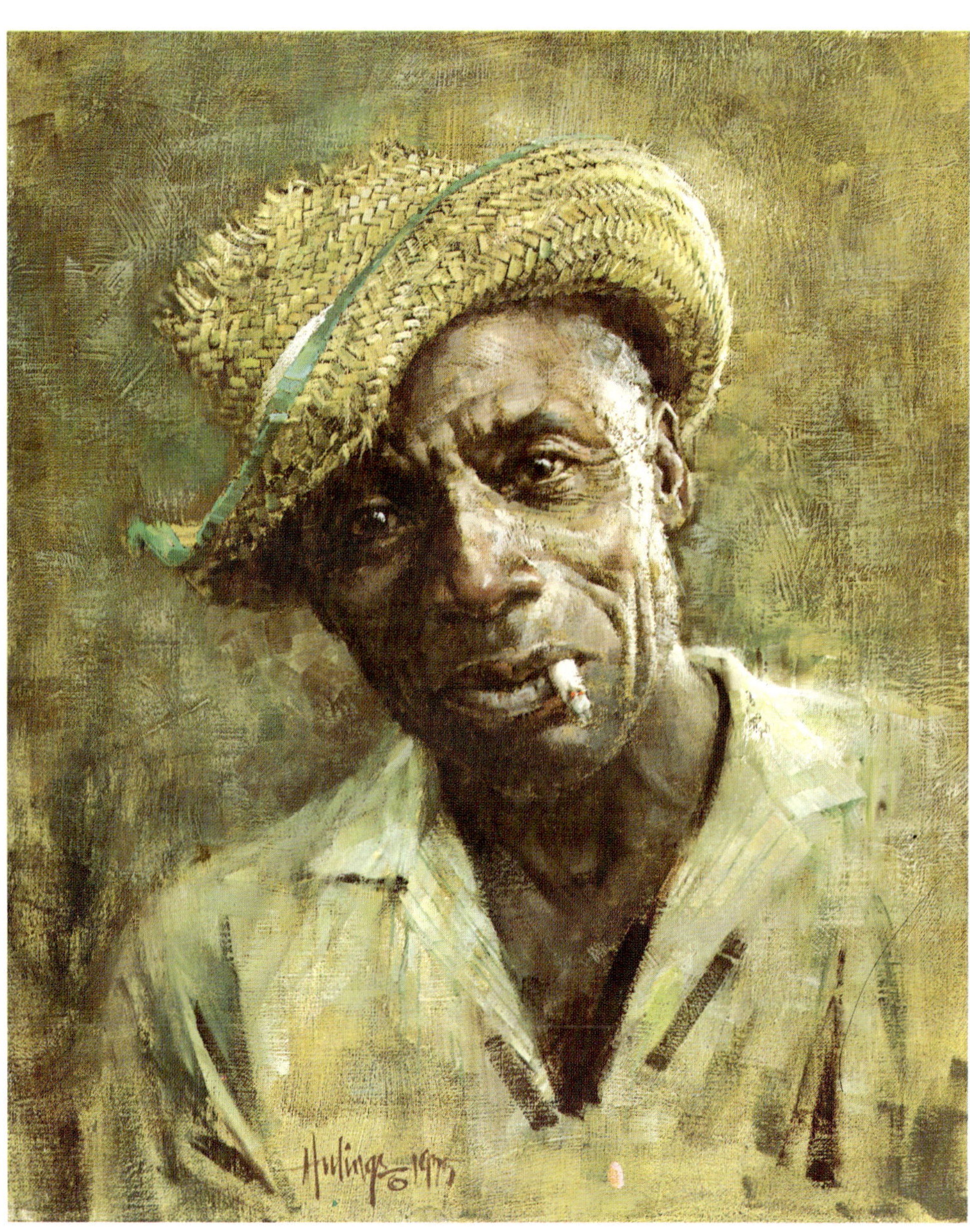

PARIS IN THE SPRING

I have painted many flower markets—in Taxco, Valencia, Florence, New York, and often in Paris. I think I like Paris best because it is a gray city—especially in the rain. The buildings are gray, the clouds are gray, the light is gray and everything is subordinated in color to the flowers themselves. Sunny days are bright and cheerful, but not colorful. Colors are their most intense on gray days. There are two challenges to be met in painting a scene such as this. First, to paint flowers of different varieties in masses so that they keep their identities as tulips, gladiolas or whatever they are, and second, to arrange and use sparingly the bright color so that the painting is not gaudy or sentimental.

Plate Fifteen 24x36 in.

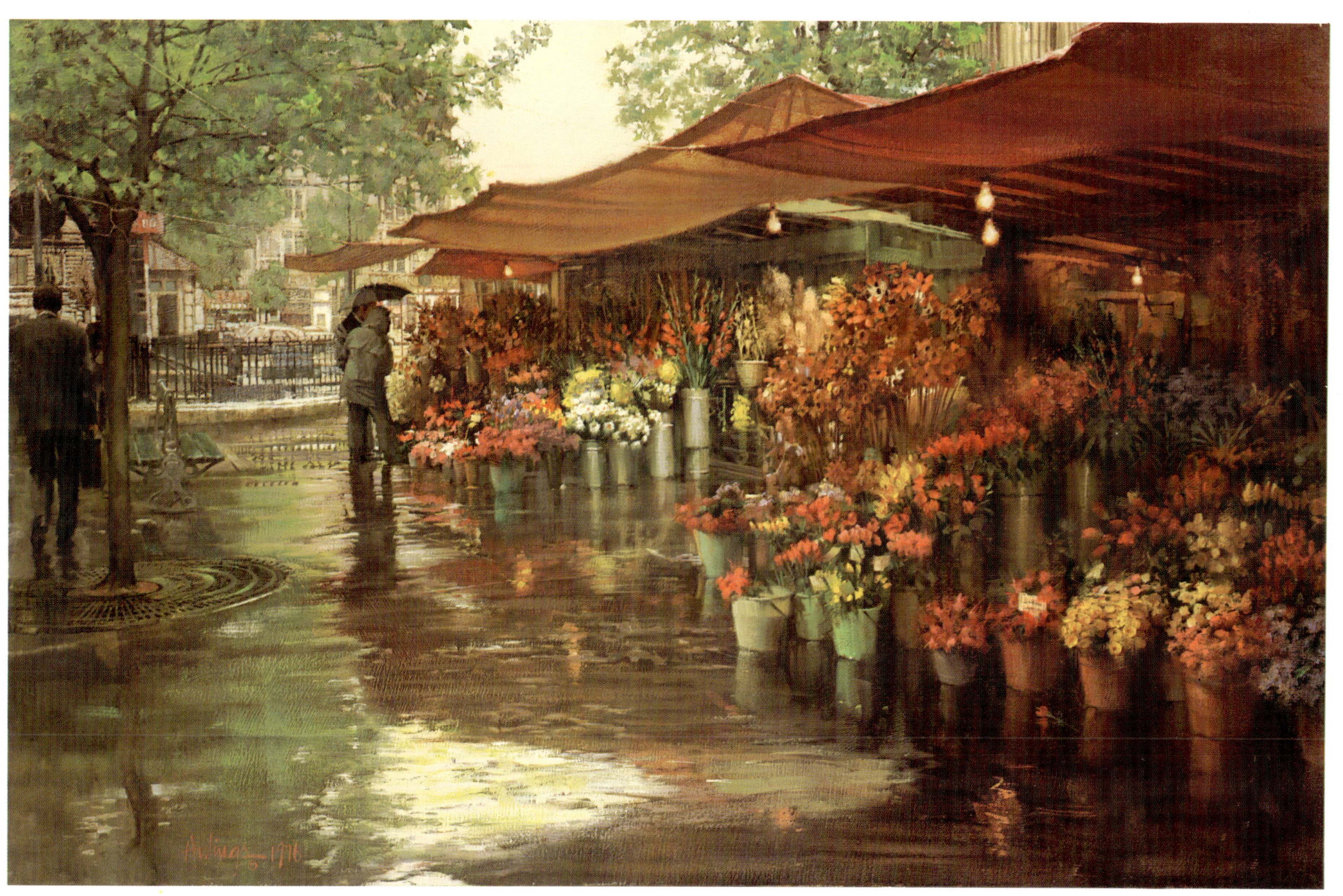

JEWISH GHETTO COURTYARD

Whenever I see anything old being destroyed, I am sorry because old things usually have a beauty of craftsmanship which is rapidly disappearing in our mechanized lives. But as I saw the tile from this patio being stacked prior to stripping and demolishing the compound, I had mixed emotions. Although I regret the passing of an age more artistic than our own, I do not mourn the end of a life that this courtyard represents. Here in Seville, as in other cities of Europe in past centuries, the Jews were forced to live in special areas and were subjected to cruel discrimination.

Plate Sixteen   20x40 in.

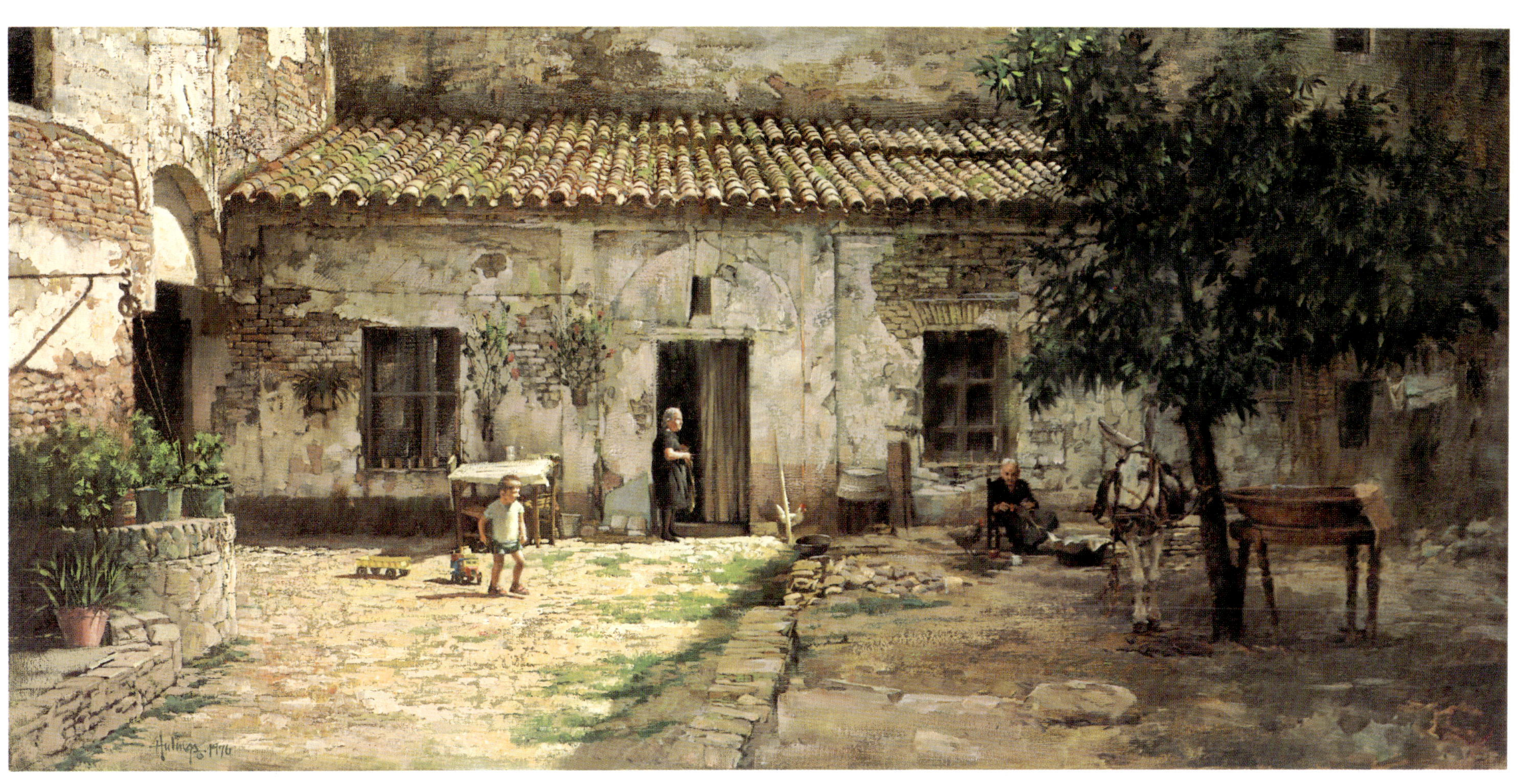

FOUR FIGURES

Inside running water has brought easier living, but it has reduced contact with friends and neighbors. Visits to the community open air laundry or water spout such as this one used to provide a little gossip and camaraderie. Where they still exist, they certainly continue to furnish excellent subject matter for artists.

Plate Seventeen 10x20 in.

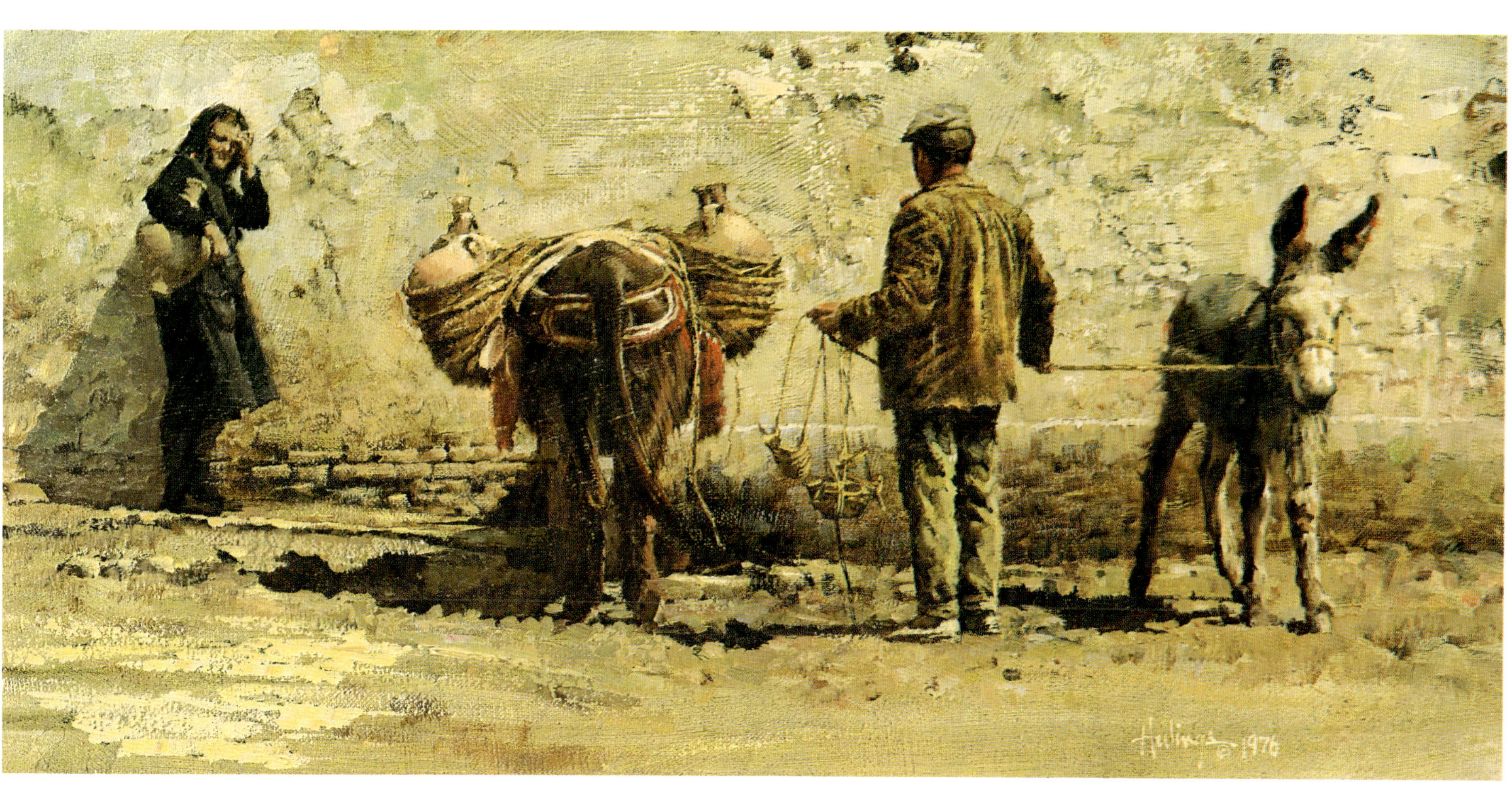
Hulings © 1976

MULE WITH PLAID BLANKET

Two of the industries on the wide plains of central Spain are sheepherding and truck farming. As long as some of the people are using draft animals, others will be manufacturing these plaid blankets to cover them. But this old cart will not long be the same. Automobile wheels with rubber tires are replacing the big, iron-banded spoked ones which cut up the new asphalt roads.

Plate Eighteen 24x36 in.

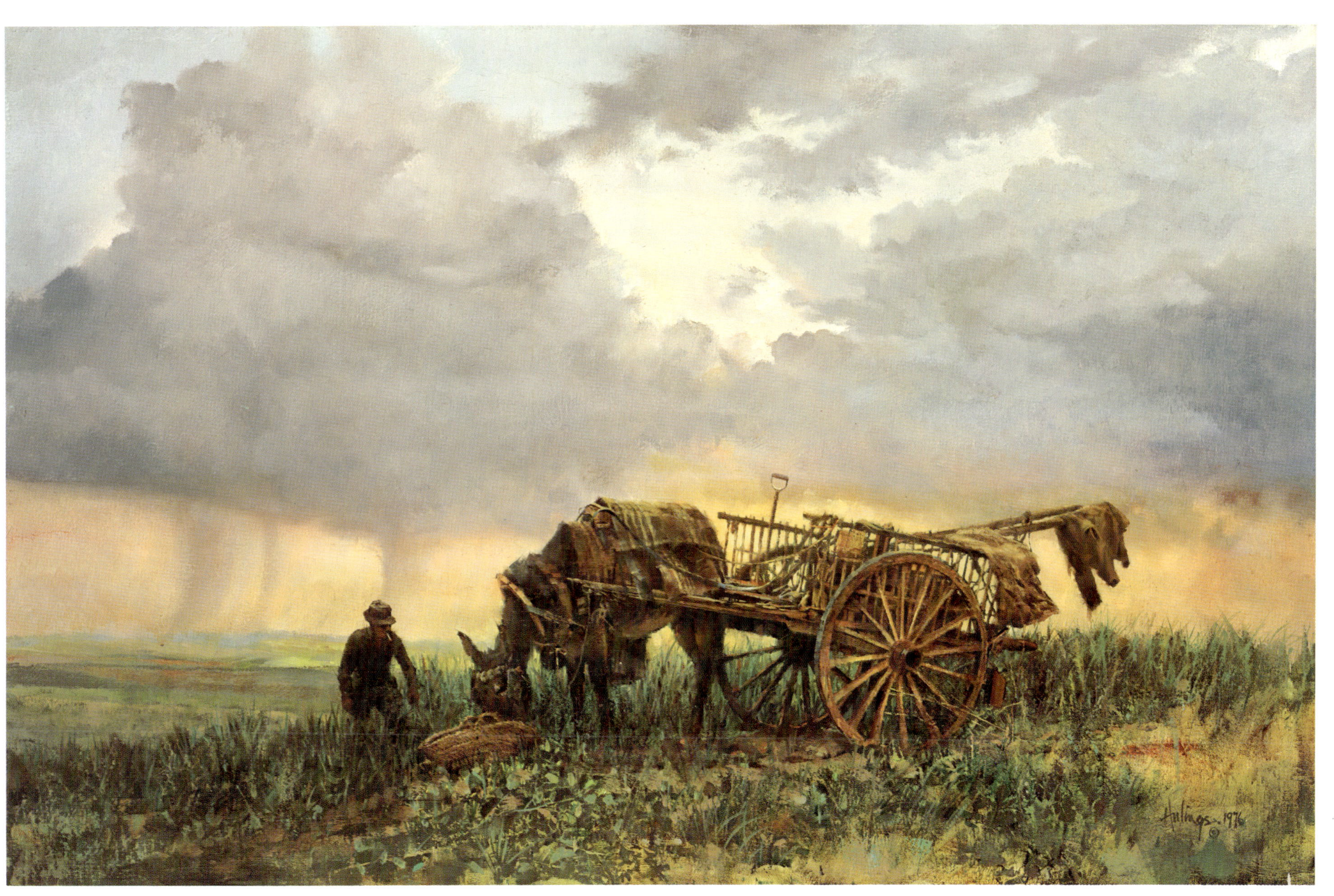
Hulings 1976

THE RED AWNING

It must be apparent to anyone seeing this collection of paintings that I enjoy trying to make order out of jumbled subject matter. It interested me to mass all those baskets and other assorted stuff into simplified patterns that hold together and to balance the light and shade values without destroying the effect of sunlight. And speaking of sunlight—it presents a problem with red. Something painted a shade of red, light enough to be in sunlight, ends up pink. Painted dark enough to be red, it ends up as if in shadow. So you get tricky and paint it partly in light and partly in shadow and let the viewer's eye figure it out.

Plate Nineteen 18x27 in.

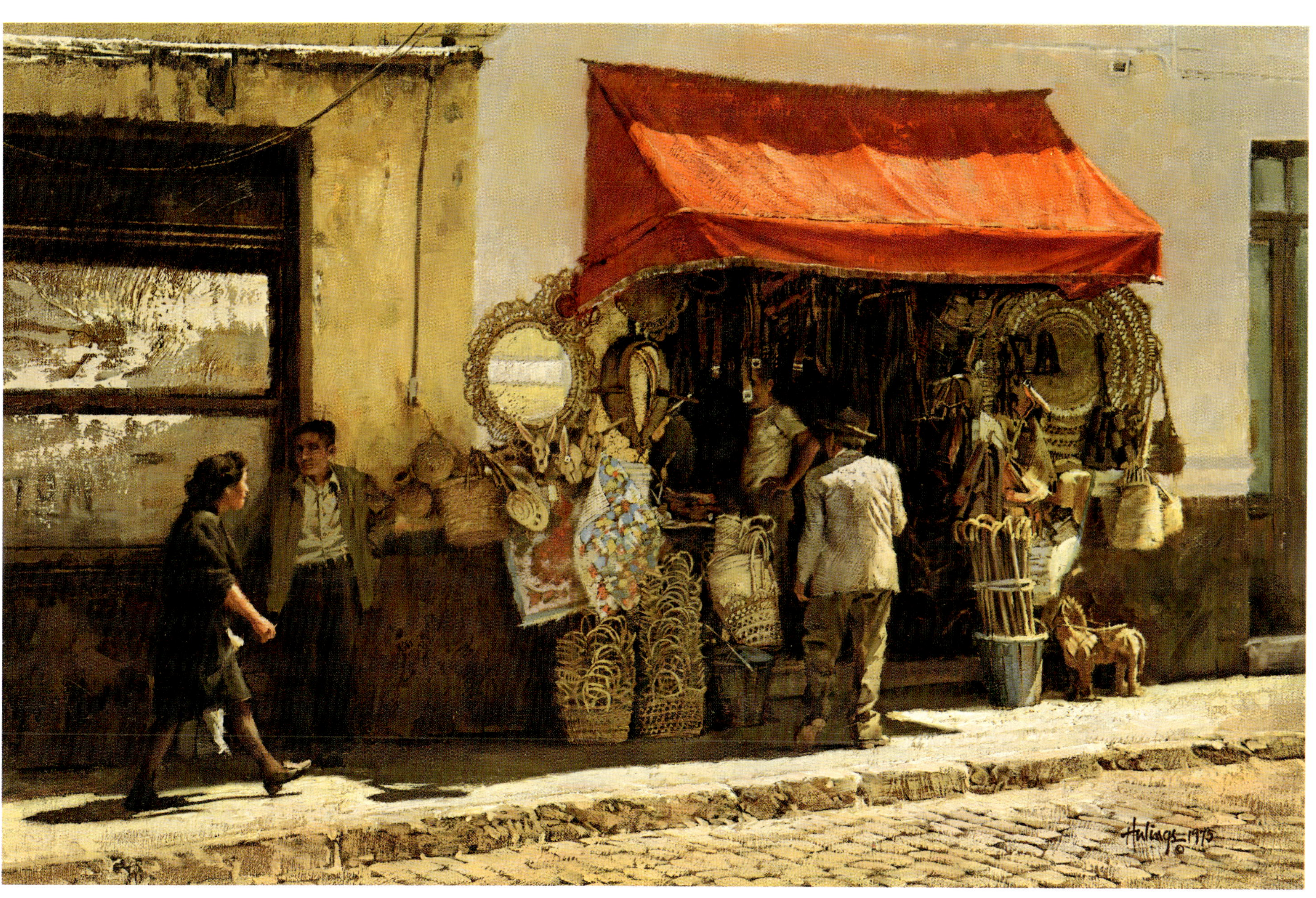
Hulings 1975 ©

TIME OUT FOR A COKE

The ever-present Coca-Cola sign beckons the thirsty all over the world. Donkeys can go long periods without drinking. Their masters can't. These animals have many characteristics that I admire. Patience is one and I love to paint them waiting. This little fellow hauls garbage. Patient and humble.

Plate Twenty 9x12 in.

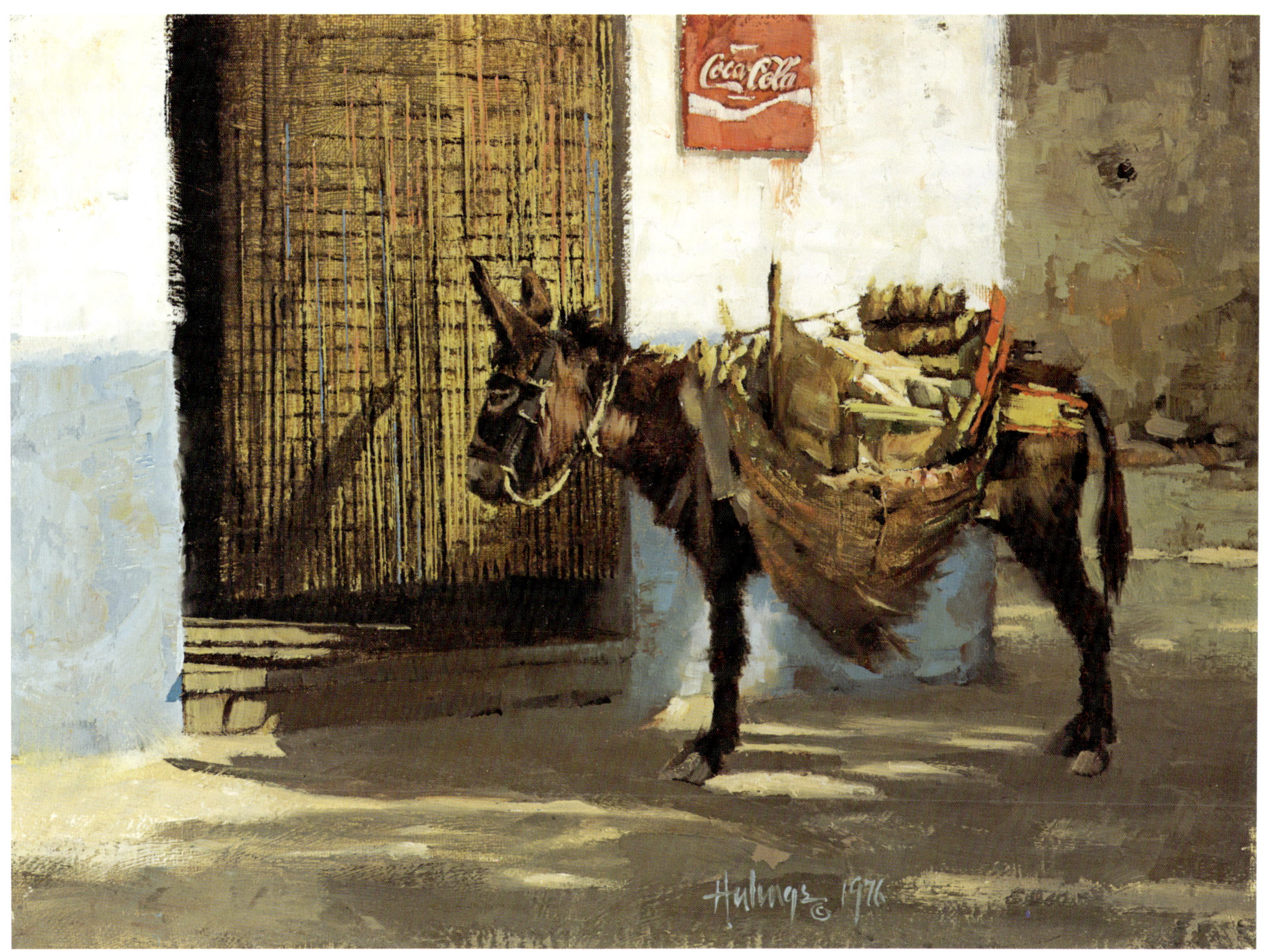
Coca-Cola
Hulings © 1976

A BOY AND HIS GRANDMOTHER

I chose this scene because it offered an interesting exercise in painting the effect of intense light. Oddly enough, such effect is achieved, not by great contrasts, but by strong reflected light in the shadow areas. The unstated principle is that the original light source must be powerful to produce so much light from reflection alone.

The composition is very simple. The two doorways in the foreground are stark accents to lock you into the center of the picture. Then the horizontal lines bisecting the buildings, the streak of light along the ground and the trickle of water all lead in perspective to the boy and his grandmother. And if that isn't enough to attract your eye, he is wearing a red shirt.

The cat is sitting there defying the rules of good composition by providing a competing center of interest. So be it! That's the way with cats.

Plate Twenty-one 20x30 in.

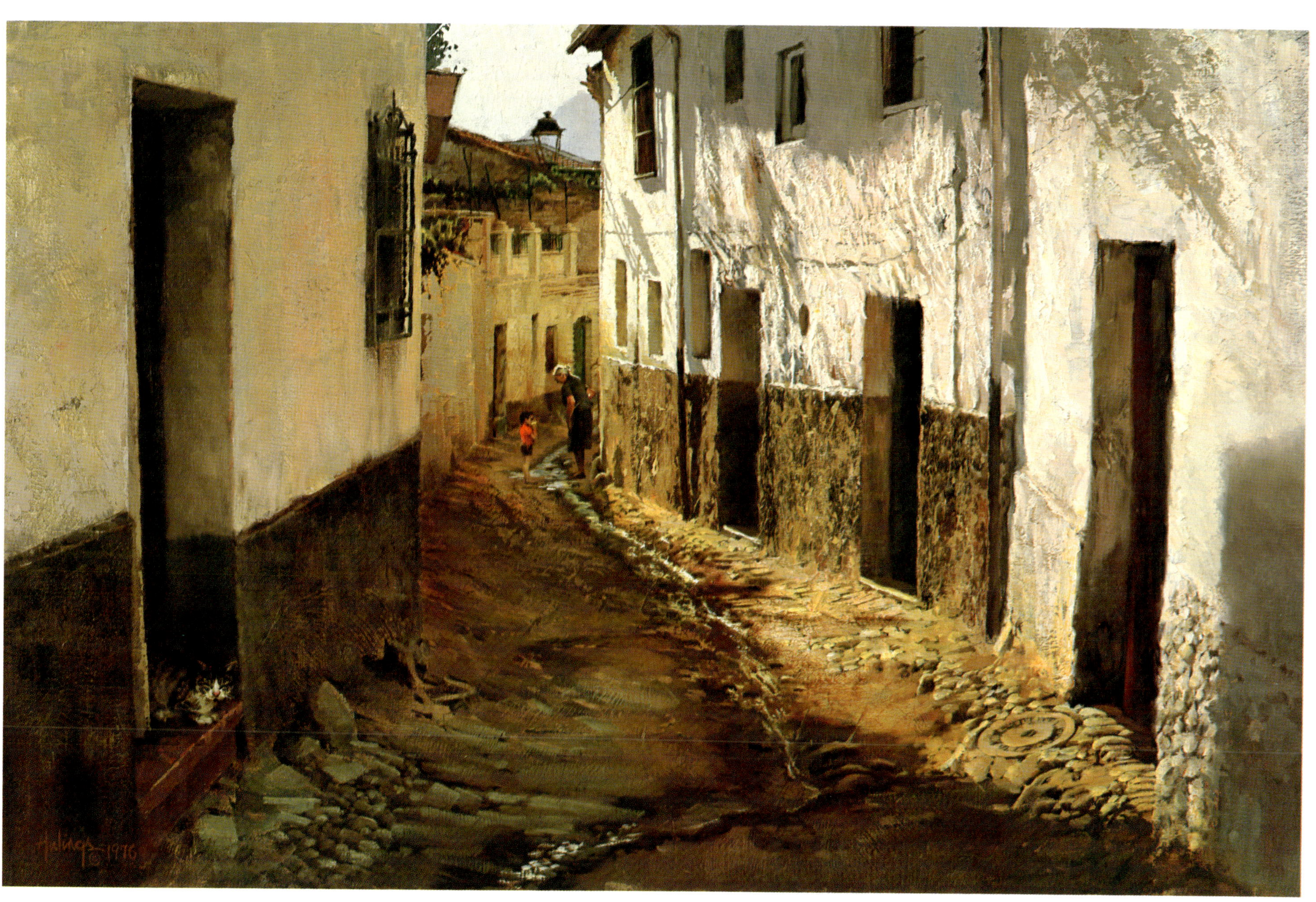

SNAPDRAGONS

After I decided to paint white and yellow snapdragons, I considered objects that would complement them. Cloth, silver, glass, fruit and china provide a pleasing variety of textures and character. The lobelia was added for sharp color contrast.

Plate Twenty-two 20x24 in.

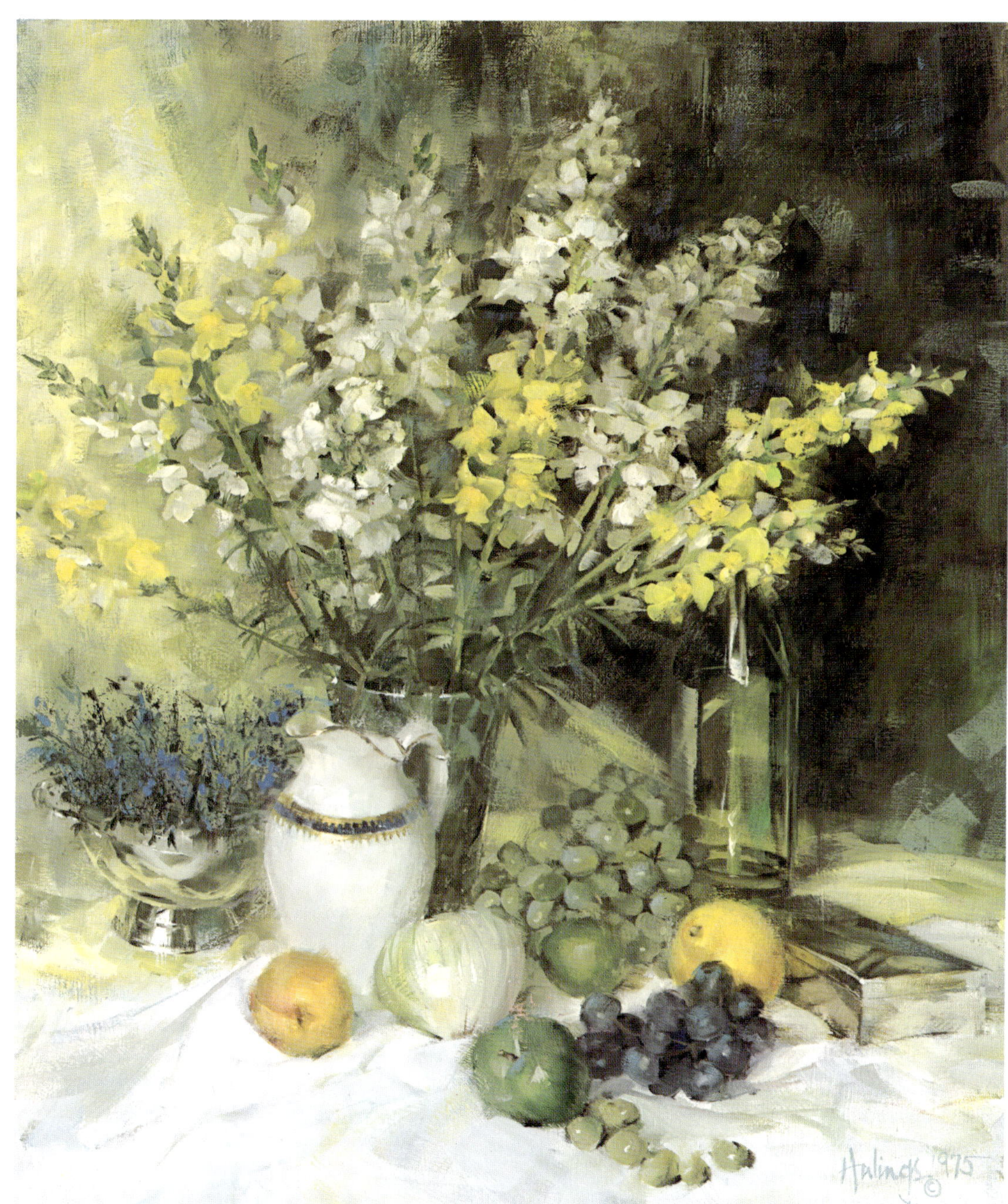

HILLTOP CONSTRUCTION SITE

An old house is being torn down to make way for a new one with a shiny tile facade. Too bad! These men are clearing away rubble. Hillside villages provide great material for abstract design and it is fun to play around with the shapes. If I ever abandon realistic painting, I will become a cubist.

Plate Twenty-three 14x21 in.

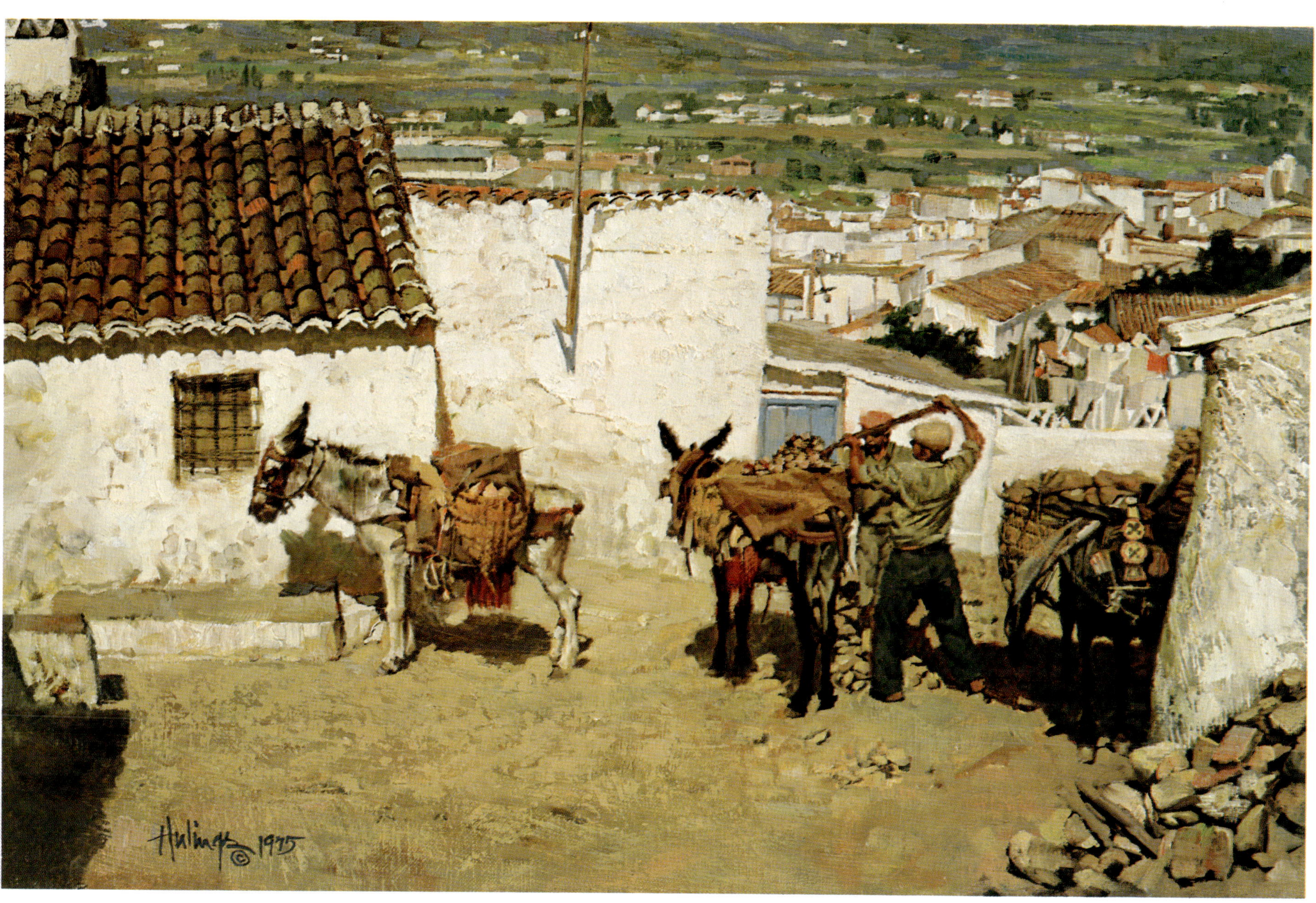

PUERTO VALLARTA

Puerto Vallarta was, until recently, a quiet fishing village connected to the rest of Mexico by a difficult road through the jungle. Now it has jet runways, luxury hotels and "muchos turistas". There is frantic building going on up in the steep hills overlooking the town and these little donkeys ply constantly back and forth with their burdens of rocks and sand from the beach. It would be selfish of me to wish these people to stay poor and unemployed simply to keep them picturesque. However, as an artist, I can't help but regret the destruction of the beautiful simplicity of their little town.

Plate Twenty-four 24x48 in.

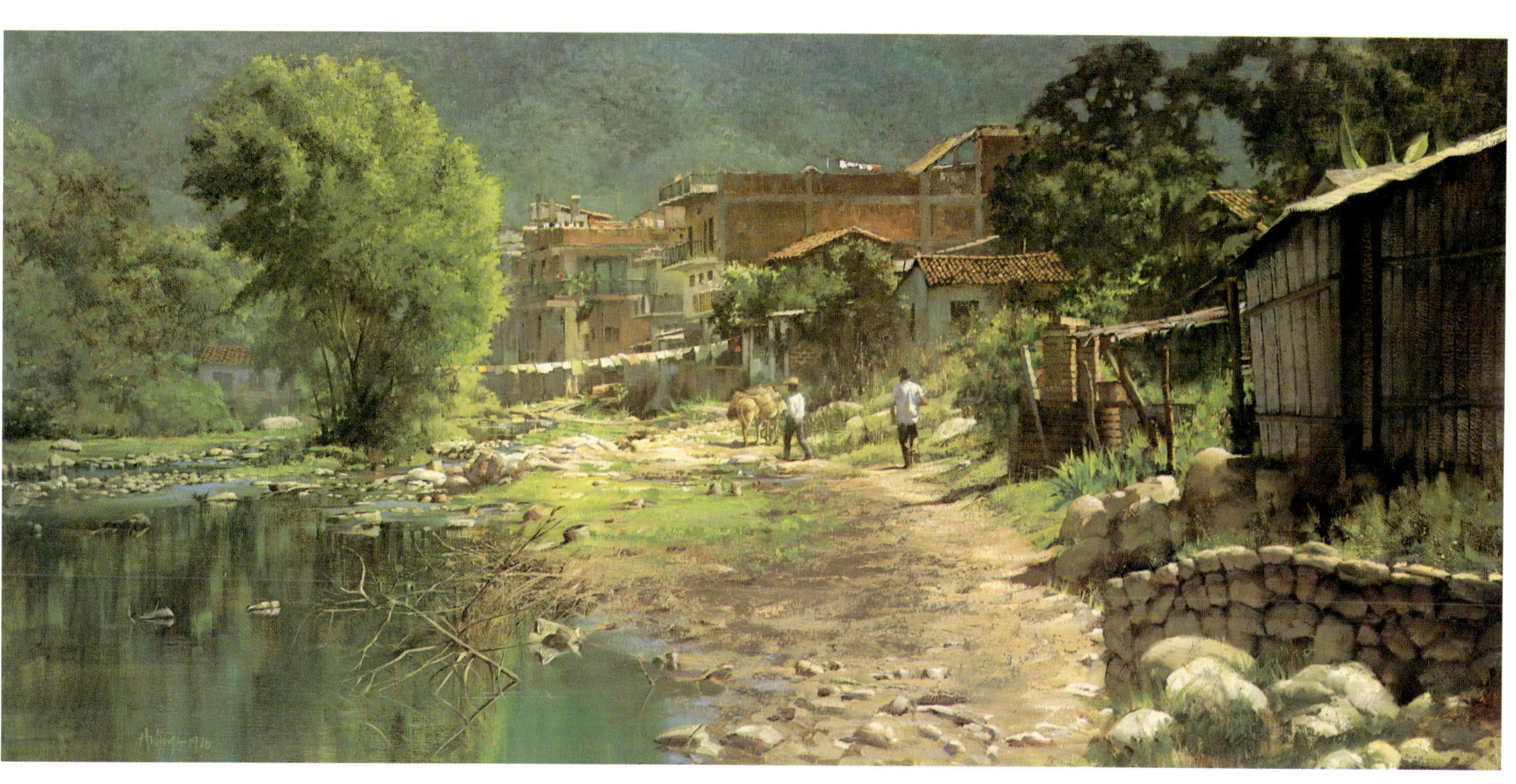

MALAGA BARRIO

If there is any truth in the notion that "Mr. Hulings' favorite challenge is to extract beauty from misery" (from a review), then this painting bears it out. How well the challenge was met is for others to judge, but it is certainly there. The crumbling walls, the tin can plant holders, the dirt road, the trash and the general slum conditions provide fascinating material. Arranged under a play of back lighting they produce an esthetic result. Perhaps if this scene were in my own country, its beauty for me would be marred by social conscience.

Plate Twenty-five 22x32 in.

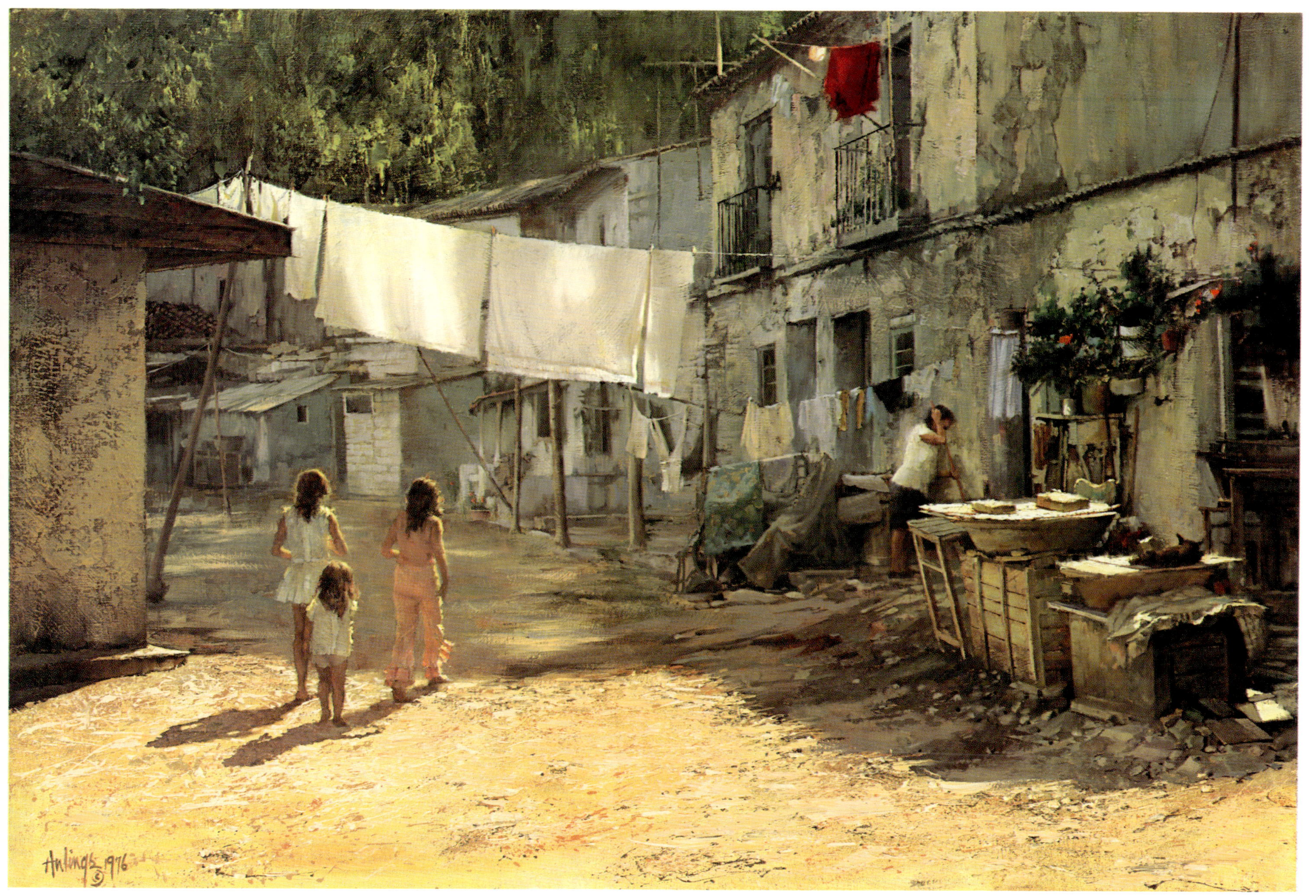
Anlings 1976 ©

GRAND CANYON, BRIGHT ANGEL TRAIL

The Grand Canyon has been a favorite subject of mine for years. In 1966 the United States Department of the Interior decided that a collection of paintings of our National Parks should be made. Various artists were invited to join in this project and it fell to me to paint the Grand Canyon. I have painted it many times since. It is certainly the ultimate challenge to a landscape artist because its scope and grandeur can only be approximated. This painting is the result of my sixth attempt.

Plate Twenty-six 24x40 in.

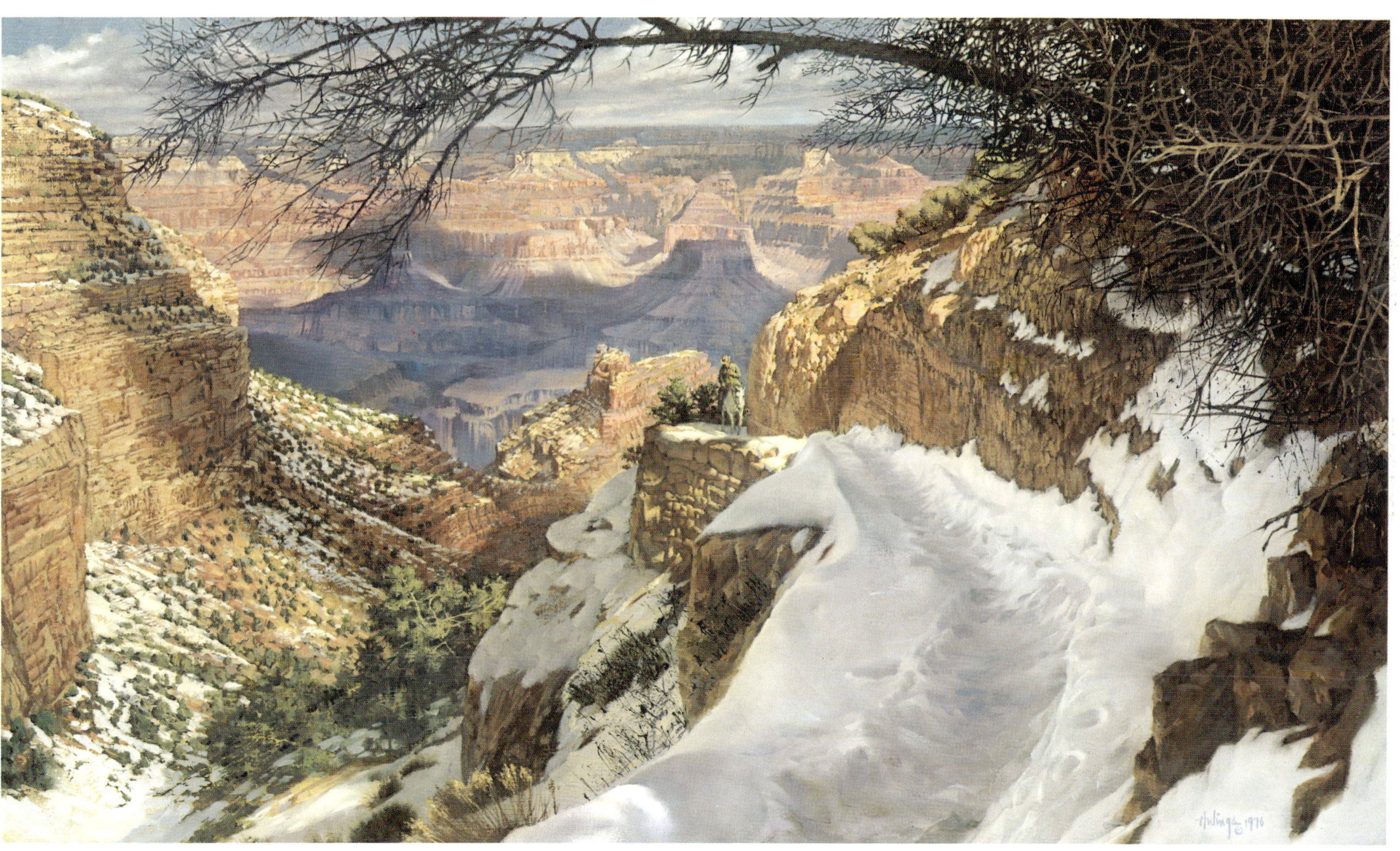

ONE PERFECT ROSE

Roses throw my summer schedule out of whack. Roses like these bloom overnight in our garden and demand to be painted "right now"! Whatever else is sitting half-finished on the easel must wait.

Plate Twenty-seven 11x12 in.

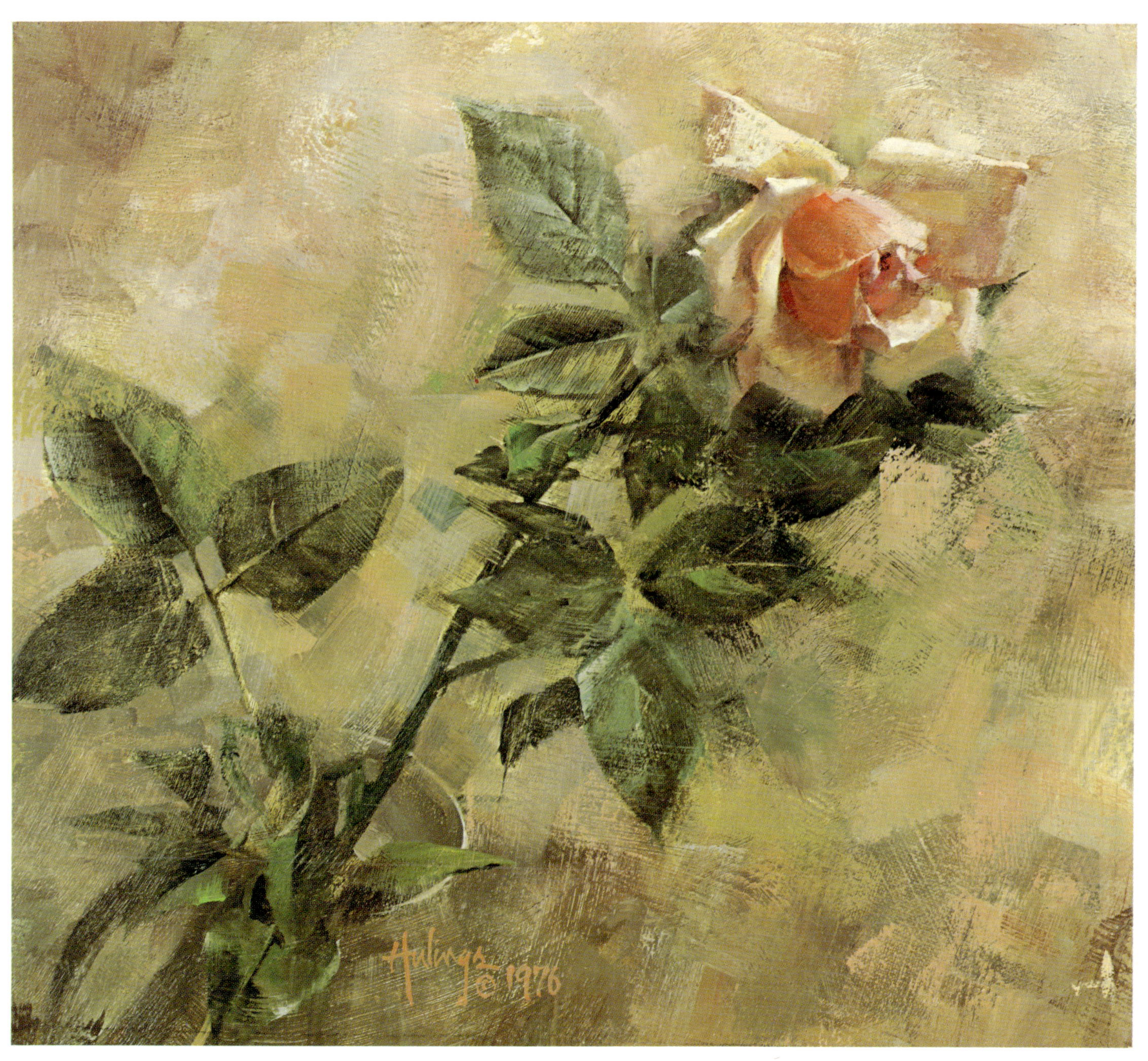
Hulings © 1976

ALHAMA

It is about 2 p.m. and the midday meal and siesta are over. It is time to return to the fields. But the sun is still hot and there's time for a short chat with an old lady.

Plate Twenty-eight 28x42 in.

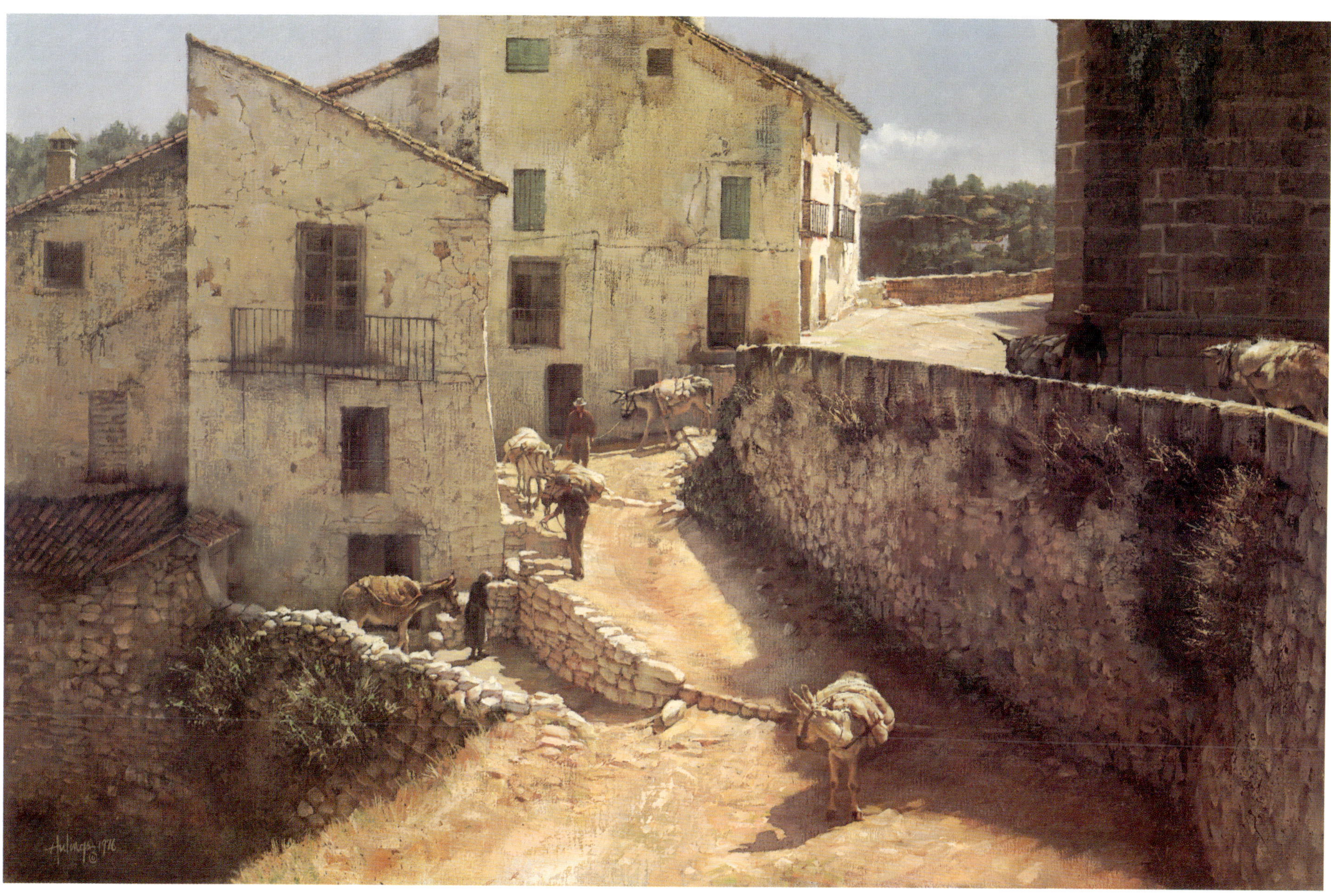

ABANDONED ADOBE

This painting was done while visiting my old friends, Dick and Edith Goetz, at their summer painting workshop in Arroyo Seco, near Taos. The village contains many picturesque but rather sad and empty little buildings crumbling in the strong New Mexico sun. Everywhere you turn there is a subject for a small painting. The chickens were added to point up the humiliation of this sturdy house that once served a proud family.

Plate Twenty-nine 14x21 in.

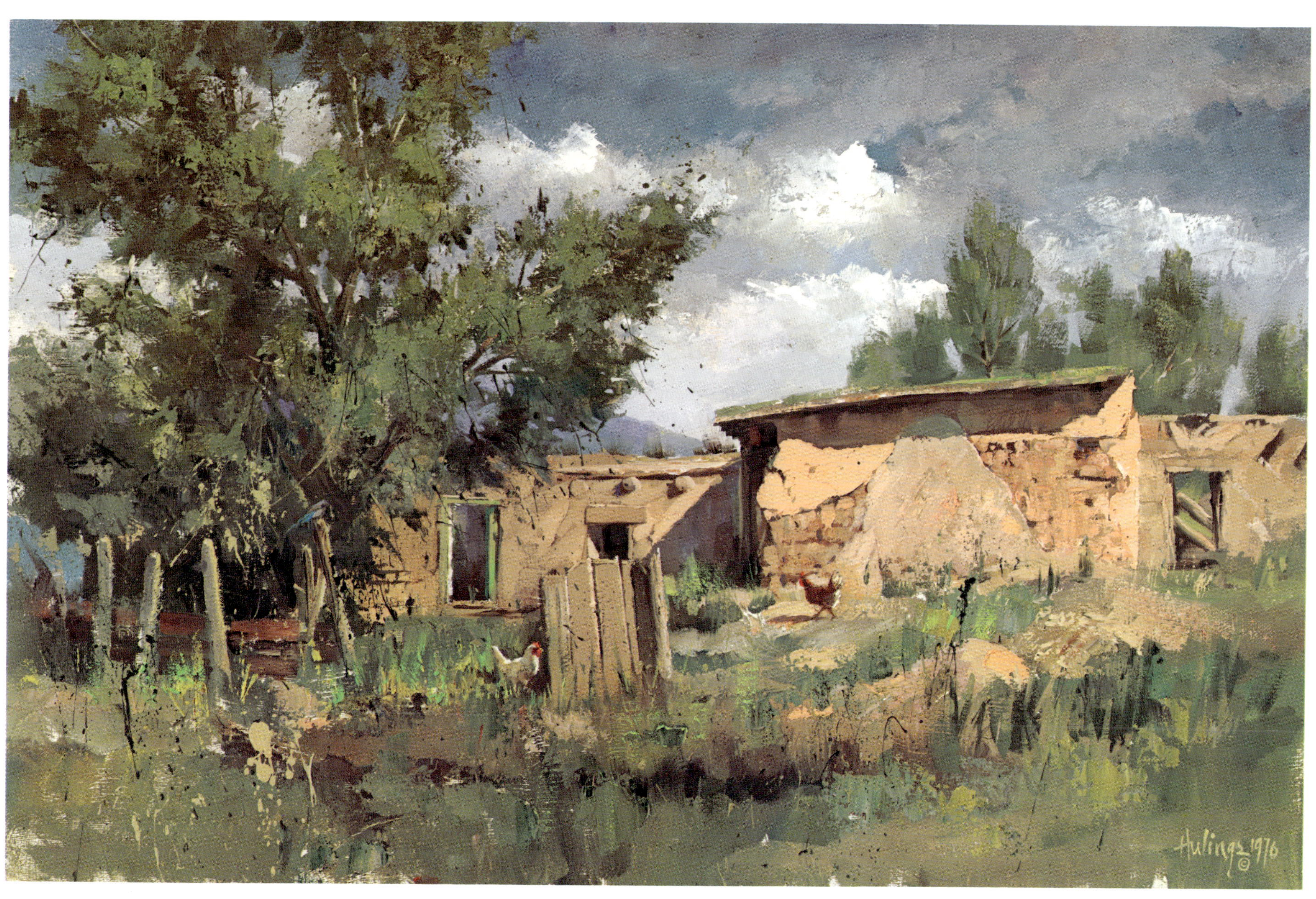
Hulings 1976
©

OLD MAN OF MEXICO

The features of this man's face might have been found on an old veteran of Coronado's army. He has had a life of poverty and hard work. Now he is resting in the shade behind the stalls at the market place awaiting the end of his struggle.

Plate Thirty 16x20 in.

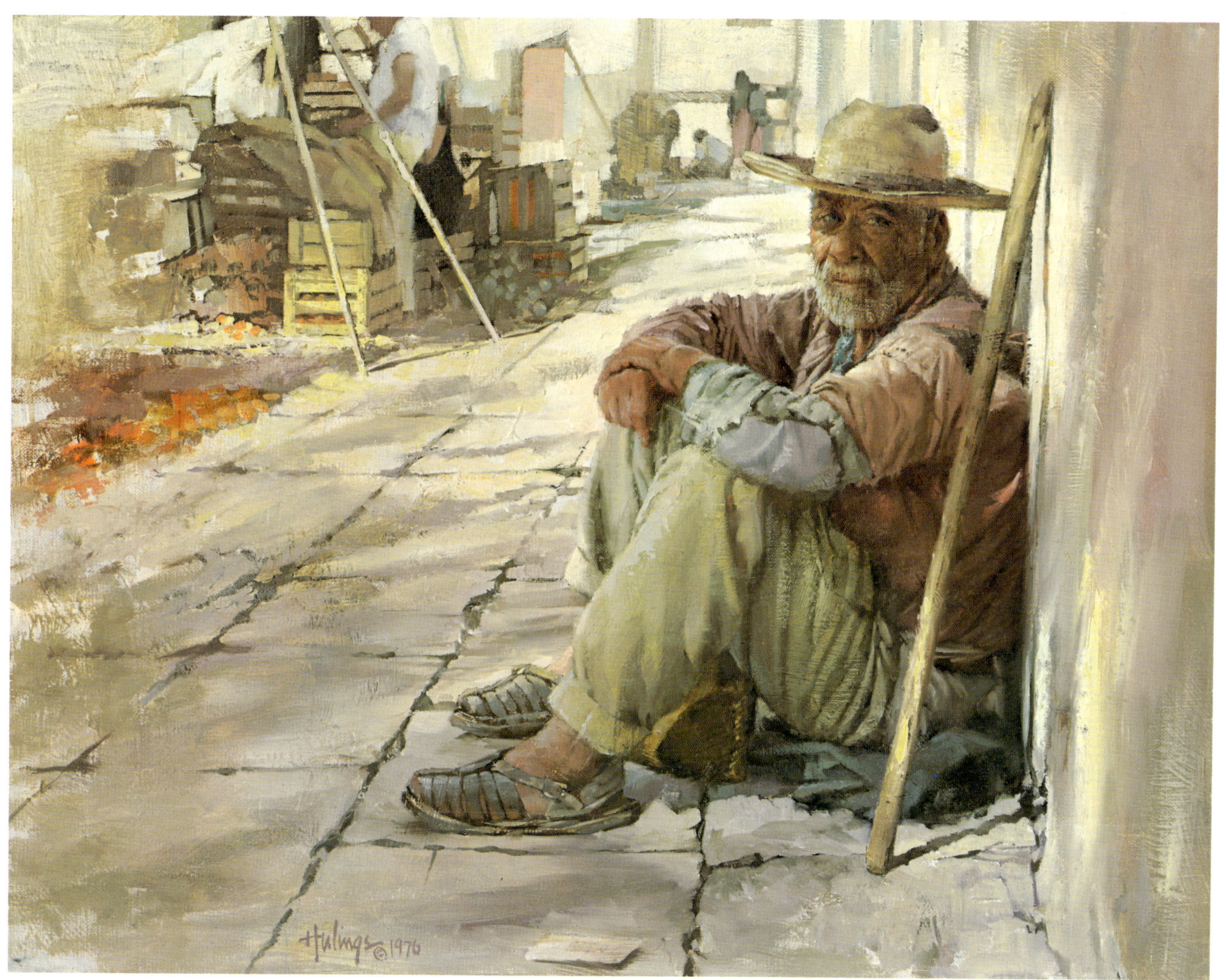
Hulings © 1976

BROWN MULE AND CART

The vertical and zigzag lines are arranged in this painting to keep pulling your eye back to the mule. The strong values and hard edges around the mule work against the diffused, pale background to produce a third dimension. The palette used is very subdued except for the red in the geranium. This creates a link between the mule and the flower. His interest is likely more gastronomic than esthetic.

Plate Thirty-one 18x24 in.

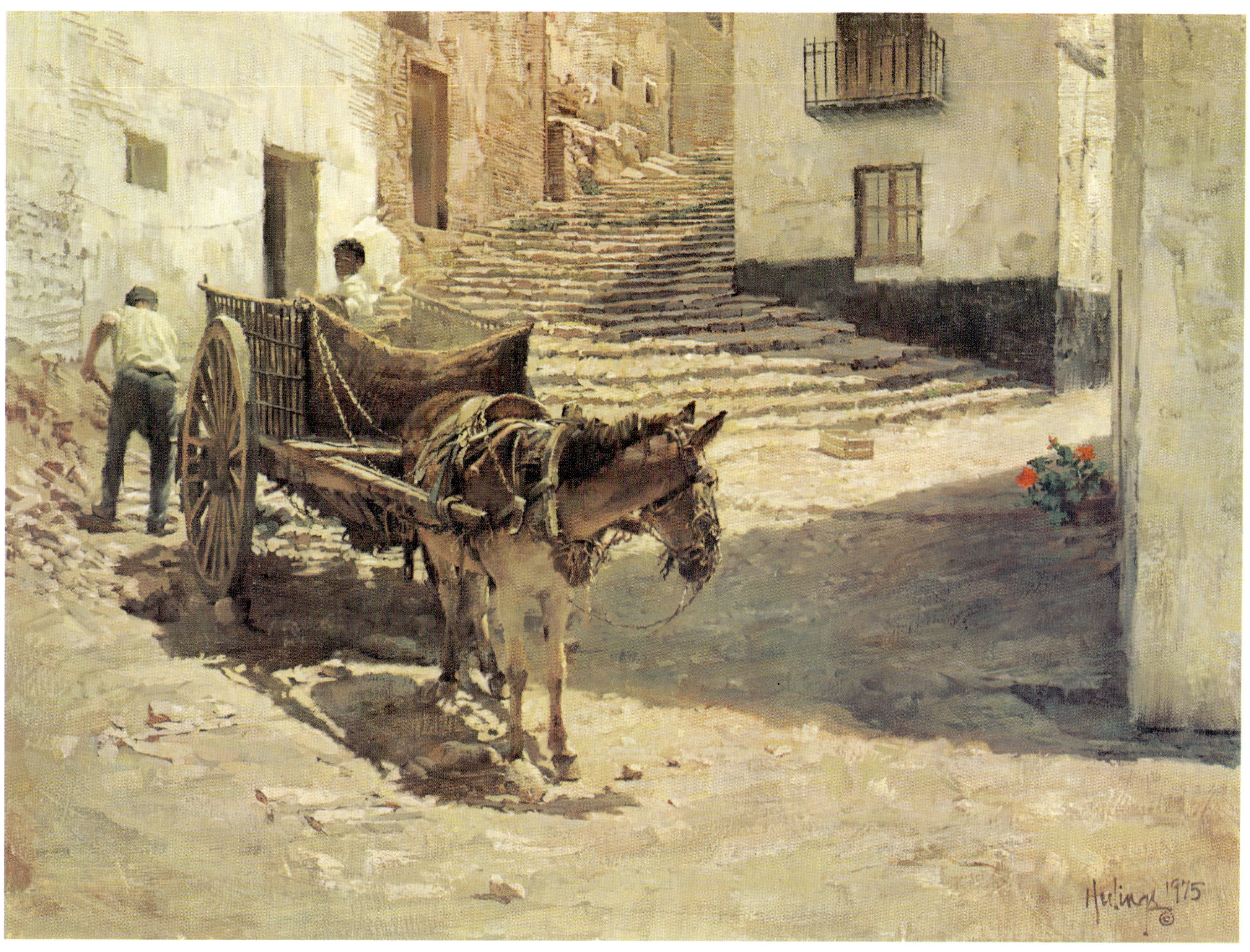

CONCENTRATION

As one looks back over the years, it is apparent that children have always appealed to artists as models. Raphael's cherubs, the little girl in Sir Joshua Reynolds' "Age of Innocence", even Picasso's circus children, are among the endless examples.

The attempt to capture their guileless charm and transparent moods can be fascinating and satisfying.

Plate Thirty-two 16x17 in.

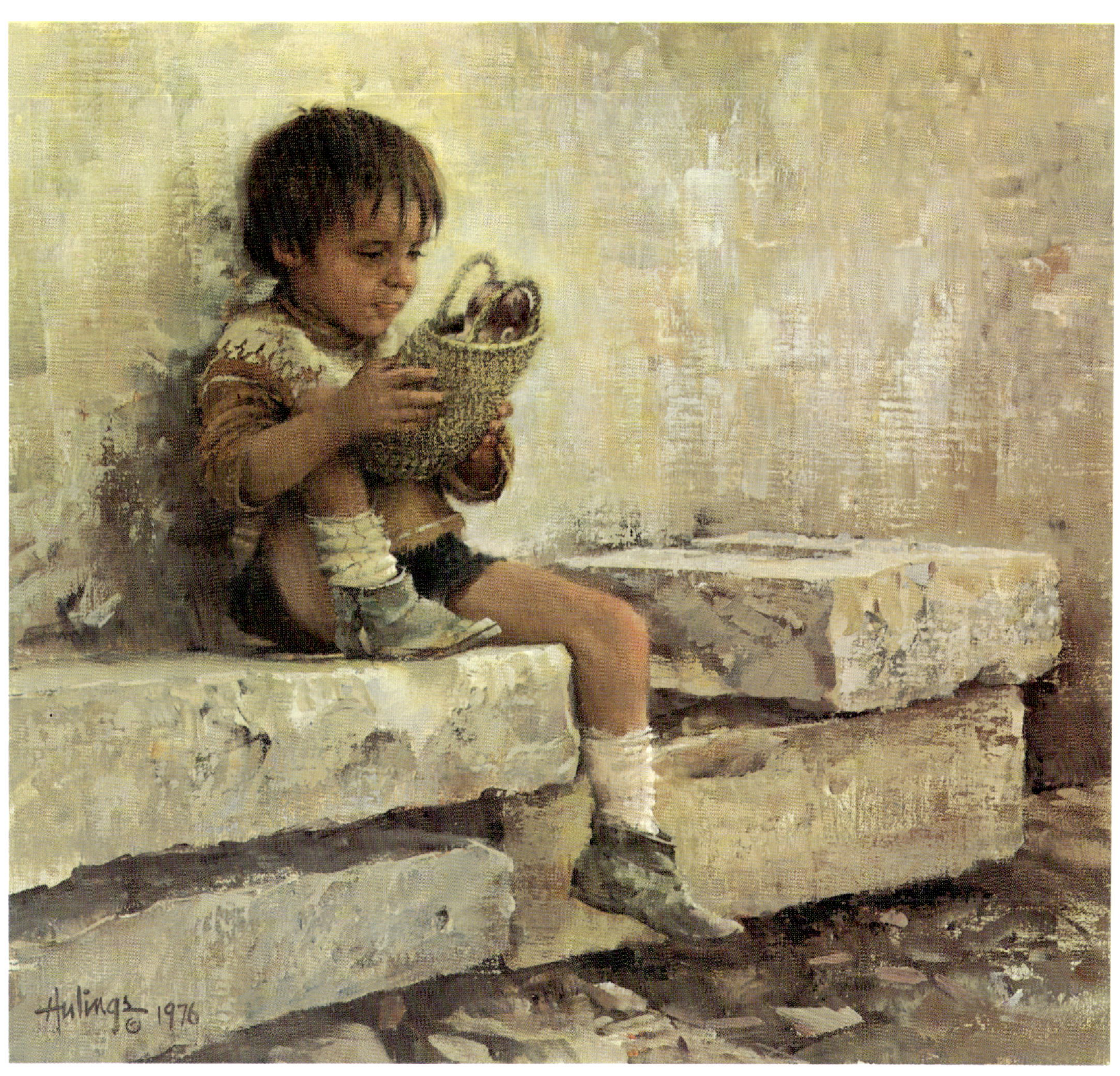
Hulings © 1976

WAITING FOR PAPA

I am generally inclined to paint a scene such as this in clear strong sunshine rather than in gray light. But it was interesting to concentrate, for a change, on the subtle local colors and the simple patterns of the tree, mule and cart placed in profile against the house. It was important that these elements be arranged to produce just the right balance of lights, darks and shapes.

An overcast day isn't ideal for a family outing. Papa had better hurry.

Plate Thirty-three 20x30 in.

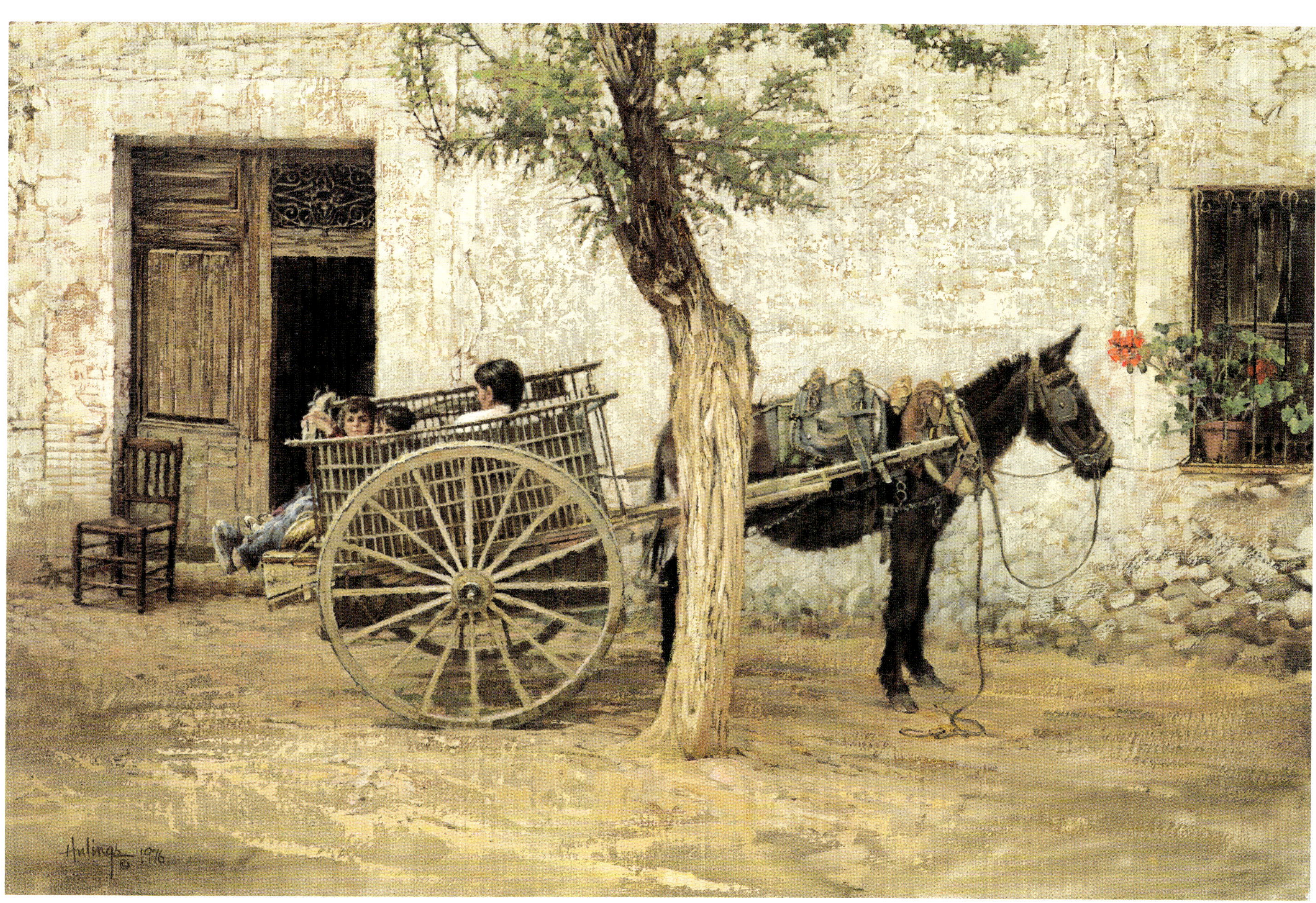

MISSISSIPPI CABIN

It is difficult for me, the artist, to say what attracted me to this scene. Perhaps it is again the challenge of finding beauty and interest in a miserable and humdrum setting. These cotton farmers are still cultivating their few acres with horses and living in the bare one-room cabin of generations ago.

I placed the house and figures in a wide horizontal composition amid empty fields and an empty white sky to convey a sense of futility.

Plate Thirty-four 10x20 in.

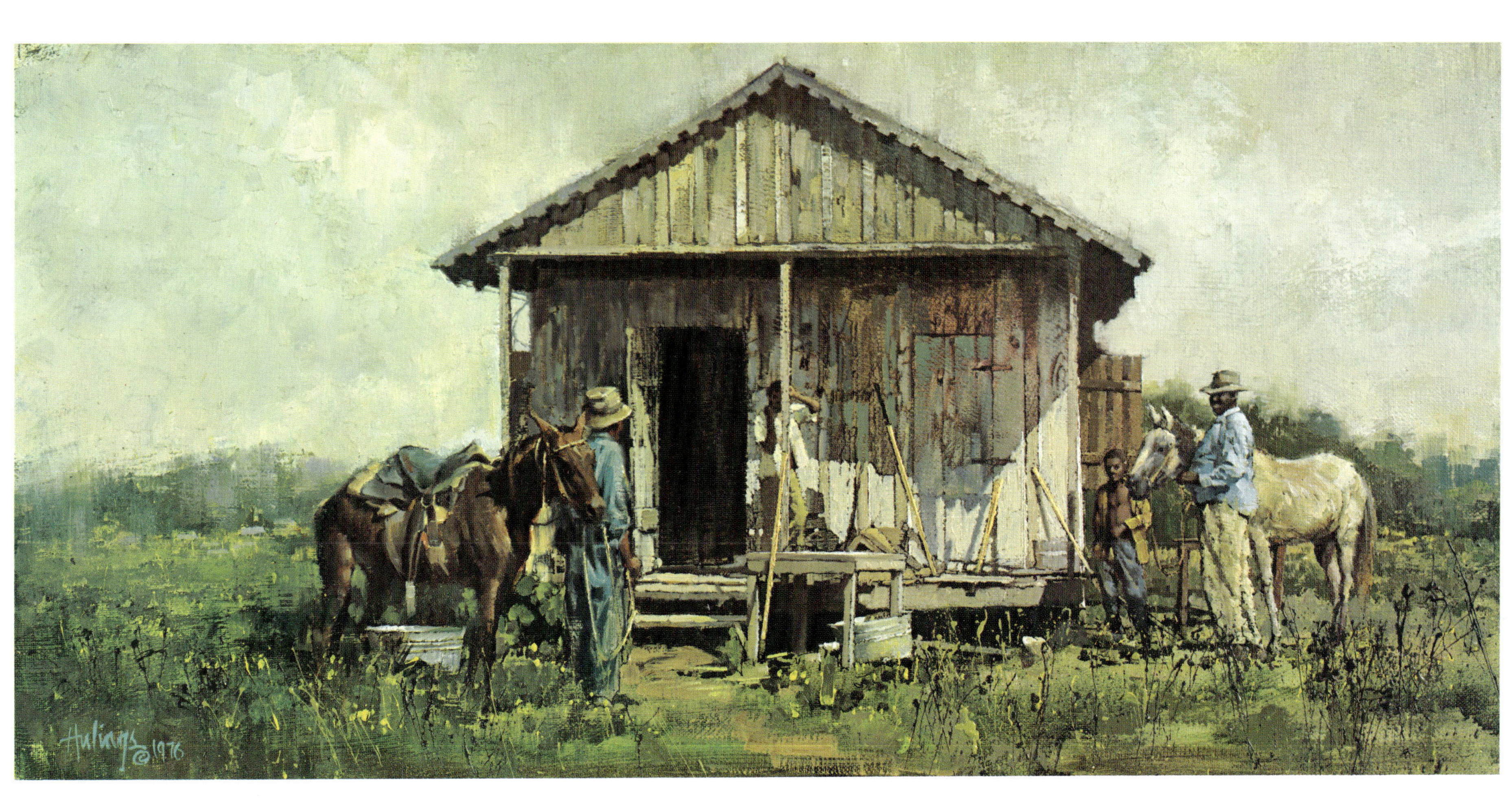
Hulings ©1976

TAOS TREES

Painting from life out-of-doors has its drawbacks. Artists have always flocked to Taos because the countryside is so paintable. The artists are part of the local color and there is open season on them for gawking and picture-taking. While I was painting this picture, a limousine stopped and one of its seven passengers approached me. Without even a "hello," he stretched out on his stomach and began taking snapshots from that "interesting angle." This done, he got up to look at my canvas. "Not bad," he said, "have you ever thought of taking up painting professionally?"

Plate Thirty-five   12x16 in.

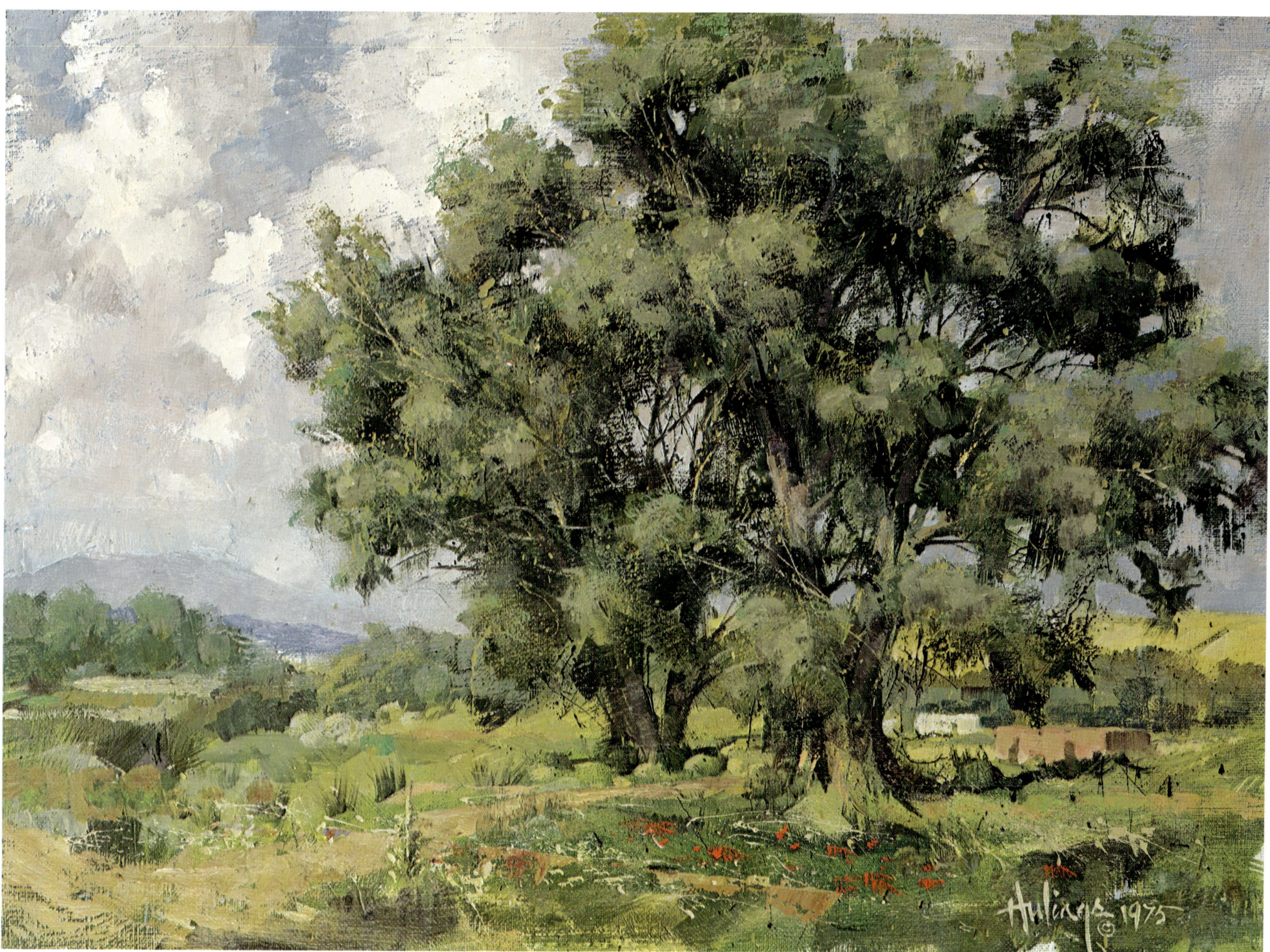

ABOUT THE ARTIST

Clark Hulings was born in 1922. His mother died when he was an infant and he lived with his maternal grandparents in Potsdam, New York, until the age of four.

His father, a chemical engineer, was sent to Valencia, Spain, to manage a plant that produced a gas for fumigating orange trees. While there he married the daughter of the British consul, and in 1926 Clark and his sister went to live with them. The children were placed in the care of a Spanish maid instructed to take them to play in a nearby park with other American and British children. However, this maid's independent nature took them instead to visit her large affectionate family surrounded by donkeys, chickens and other "local color."

Two years in that sunny country of whitewashed houses, dusty colors and the ubiquitous donkey produced a nostalgia which perhaps today explains not only his choice of subject matter, but also his fascination with brilliant light—a fascination which caused Patricia Boyd Wilson, art critic for the *Christian Science Monitor,* to say: "Hulings' particular talent goes beyond the mere definition of light and describes the air itself."

Once back in the United States, the family settled in Westfield, New Jersey. Clark attended twelve years of public school. During the first ten there was little evidence of any special aptitude for painting. At the age of fifteen, however, the boy was given a small box of oil paints and he began copying with great accuracy paintings around the house—mostly Spanish village scenes.

Although Clark's father had no creative talents in the field of painting, he had always been interested in it and was an ardent visitor to art museums. It was at this time, as his son's natural ability and dedication became more apparent, that a great aunt fell seriously ill. Her illness necessitated frequent visits to her home near the

Metropolitan Museum of Art, providing the boy with an opportunity for inspiration and study of some of the world's greatest paintings. The hours spent at the museum were supplemented by practical weekend art lessons at home.

Fortunately, there lived in Westfield a fine painter and gifted teacher named Sigismund Ivanowski. Ivanowski had been a young man in Paris when the French Impressionists were at their creative peaks. The influence of these free spirits was exerted over a foundation of rigid training acquired in the academic schools of Warsaw and St. Petersburg. He believed that a painter should first train the hand to obey the brain, much as does the concert pianist, so that the interpretation of nature and creative expression do not suffer from the limitations of mere technical ineptitude. Purposeful flights of fancy and experiments in abstraction were tolerated and even encouraged, but never at the expense of craftsmanship. This point of view was impressed on young Hulings during his lessons.

Upon Clark's graduation from high school in 1940, ill health required a year's rest. he continued to study with Ivanowski every morning and, in addition, commuted to the Art Students' League in the afternoons for classes in drawing and anatomy with George Bridgeman.

In the fall of 1941 he entered Haverford College. Up to this point there had been little serious talk about career. Clark regarded the study of painting as the basis for his life's work, while his father treated it as development of a talent to be used as a hobby. The depression years had not been kind to artists and even one so great as Ivanowski was experiencing difficult times. Hulings graduated in 1944 with a degree in physics and a job with the mysterious Manhattan Project. However, poor health interrupted his plan and he went to the dry climate of Sante Fe, New Mexico, to recuperate. Painting filled the empty hours. Before long he was supporting himself, painting pastel portraits of children. In the spring of 1945 he had a one-man show of his landscapes at the New Mexico Art Museum in Santa Fe. Shortly thereafter he went to work briefly in a laboratory in Denver, Colorado. He spent his day off every week in the mountains painting landscapes and his evenings in drawing classes at Denver University.

In 1946, while visiting his parents in Louisiana, he embarked on a successful career in portrait painting, which led to a one-man show at the Louisiana Art Commission. During this period he continued to paint landscapes and also became interested in illustration and design. Such interest took him back to New York City and the Art Students' League—this time to study with Frank Reilly.

In 1951 Hulings began a commercial career in an art studio doing wash drawings of hams, turkeys and holiday decorations for a newspaper mat agency that specialized in ads for supermarkets. In his spare time he worked on samples which led to a free-lance career painting covers for paperback books and record albums and illustrations for adventure magazines. This business is demanding. To be successful, it is necessary to become versatile in technique, media and subject matter. One must learn to work well from all kinds of reference material as well as imagination and to design around type areas and page shapes. Also, one must learn to simplify and exaggerate to produce an immediate impact and to accommodate the limitations of reproduction. The rigid deadlines of the publishing business developed working habits and self-discipline which have been useful to Hulings ever since.

The struggle of these years of school and commercial illustration was supported by frequent visits to Louisiana to execute portrait commissions. By 1956 Hulings' career as an illustrator was firmly established. But the constant lure of landscape painting sent him on a visit to Europe. This happy time was spent wandering through picture galleries and painting out in the open. Approaching winter forced him further and further south—all the way to Sicily, where he rediscovered sun-baked villages and donkeys.

After four months, conscience and duty called him back to his New York work.

But the call was not very strong and less than two years later he packed up in earnest and left for Europe—this time for a stay which lasted three years.

Hulings spent this time freely practicing his skills, developing his talent and whimsically experimenting in an atmosphere unrestricted by the needs of satisfying an art director. He roamed from the Arctic Circle to southern Egypt visiting picture galleries and doing drawings and water colors from the front seat of his car. But he was also learning to look for, to see and to compose pictures. Many months were spent in Germany studying design, in Italy studying the human figure and Renaissance art, and in Spain just painting. Throughout these travels, he constantly used the camera and began the collection of pictures which provide reference material for his paintings.

In the fall of 1960 he returned to New York City and again resumed his illustration career. But now these assignments began to be interspersed with serious landscape paintings. The paintings began to sell and within two years this new pursuit became not only more satisfying but economically more profitable than illustration, and he decided to devote all his attention to it. Since 1962 demand for Clark Hulings paintings has steadily increased.

In 1966 he married the former Mary Belfi and their daughter Elizabeth was born two years later. When they are not traveling, they live in Sante Fe.

INDEX OF ILLUSTRATIONS

HULINGS

A Collection of Oil Paintings by Clark Hulings

was designed by David E. Spaw,
photocomposed in Trump Mediaeval,
and printed on Warren's Flokote Enamel
by
The Lowell Press, Kansas City, Missouri